BARBADOS

THE MINI ROUGH GUIDE

There are more than one hundred and fifty Rough
Guide travel, phrasebook, and music titles,
covering destinations from Amsterdam to
Zimbabwe, languages from Czech to Vietnamese,
and musics from World to Opera and Jazz

Forthcoming titles include

Devon & Cornwall • Madeira • Tenerife • Vancouver

Rough Guides on the Internet

www.roughguides.com

Rough Guide Credits

Text editor: Chris Schüler. Series editor: Mark Ellingham
Production: Helen Ostick
Cartography: Melissa Baker, Maxine Repath

Publishing Information

This first edition published October 1998 by
Rough Guides Ltd, 62–70 Shorts Gardens, London, WC2H 9AH
Reprinted August 1999 & January 2001.

Distributed by the Penguin Group:
Penguin Books Ltd, 27 Wrights Lane, London W8 5TZ
Penguin Putnam Inc., 375 Hudson Street, New York 10014, USA
Penguin Books Australia Ltd, 487 Maroondah Highway,
PO Box 257, Ringwood, Victoria 3134, Australia
Penguin Books Canada Ltd, 10 Alcorn Avenue,
Toronto, Ontario, Canada M4V 1E4
Penguin Books (NZ) Ltd, 182–190 Wairau Road,
Auckland 10, New Zealand

Typeset in Bembo and Helvetica to an original design by Henry Iles.
Printed in Spain by Graphy Cems.

© Adam Vaitilingam 240pp, includes index
A catalogue record for this book is available from the British Library.
ISBN 1-85828-328-0

BARBADOS

THE MINI ROUGH GUIDE

by Adam Vaitilingam

ROUGH GUIDES

We set out to do something different when the first Rough Guide was published in 1982. Mark Ellingham, just out of university, was travelling in Greece. He brought along the popular guides of the day, but found they were all lacking in some way. They were either strong on ruins and museums but went on for pages without mentioning a beach or taverna. Or they were so conscious of the need to save money that they lost sight of Greece's cultural and historical significance. Also, none of the books told him anything about Greece's contemporary life – its politics, its culture, its people, and how they lived.

So with no job in prospect, Mark decided to write his own guidebook, one which aimed to provide practical information that was second to none, detailing the best beaches and the hottest clubs and restaurants, while also giving hard-hitting accounts of every sight, both famous and obscure, and providing up-to-the-minute information on contemporary culture. It was a guide that encouraged independent travellers to find the best of Greece, and was a great success, getting shortlisted for the Thomas Cook travel guide award, and encouraging Mark, along with three friends, to expand the series.

The Rough Guide list grew rapidly and the letters flooded in, indicating a much broader readership than had been anticipated, but one which uniformly appreciated the Rough Guide mix of practical detail and humour, irreverence and enthusiasm. Things haven't changed. The same four friends who began the series are still the caretakers of the Rough Guide mission today: to provide the most reliable, up-to-date and entertaining information to independent-minded travellers of all ages, on all budgets.

We now publish more than 100 titles and have offices in London and New York. The travel guides are written and researched by a dedicated team of more than 100 authors, based in Britain, Europe, the USA and Australia. We have also created a unique series of phrasebooks to accompany the travel series, along with an acclaimed series of music guides, and a best-selling pocket guide to the Internet and World Wide Web. We also publish comprehensive travel information on our Web site: **www.roughguides.com**

Help Us Update

We've gone to a lot of effort to ensure that this first edition of *The Rough Guide to Barbados* is as up to date and accurate as possible. However, if you feel there are places we've underrated or over-praised, or find we've missed something good or covered something which has now gone, then please write: suggestions, comments or corrections are much appreciated.

We'll credit all contributions, and send a copy of the next edition (or any other Rough Guide if you prefer) for the best letters. Please mark letters: "Rough Guide Barbados Update" and send to:

Rough Guides, 62–70 Shorts Gardens, London, WC2H 9AH, or Rough Guides, 375 Hudson St, 4th Floor, New York NY 10014.

Or send email to: mail@roughguides.co.uk
Online updates about this book can be found on
Rough Guides' Web site (see opposite)

The Author

Adam Vaitilingam is a barrister, freelance writer and occasional sax player who lived in the West Indies from 1989 to 1993. He is author of the *Mini Rough Guide to Antigua* and co-author of the *Rough Guide to Jamaica*.

Acknowledgements

Thanks to everyone at the Barbados Tourism Authority in London and Bridgetown, Toni at Crystal Waters, and Sandy & Suku.

CONTENTS

Contexts

INTRODUCTION

Tourists pour into Barbados from all over the world, drawn by the delightful climate, the big blue sea and brilliant white sandy beaches. Many of them rarely stray far from their hotels and guesthouses, but those who make an effort find a proud island scattered with an impressive range of historic sites and, away from the mostly gently rolling landscape, dramatic scenery in hidden caves, cliffs and gullies.

Chief among the island's attractions are its old plantation houses – places like St Nicholas Abbey and Francia – superb botanical gardens at Andromeda and the Flower Forest, and the military forts and signal stations at Gun Hill and Grenade Hall. The capital Bridgetown is a lively place to visit, with an excellent national museum and great nightlife in its bars and clubs, some of them located right on the beach. No other town begins to approach the capital

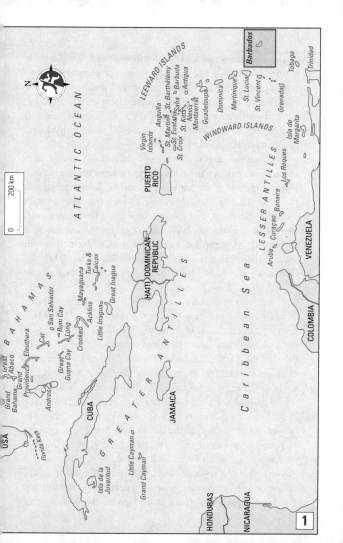

in size, but the small and largely untouristed Speightstown – once a thriving and wealthy port – is a good place to wander for a couple of hours then grab a drink on a terrace overlooking the sea. And, of course, there are the beaches, from the often crowded strips such as Accra Beach and Mullins Bay to tiny but superb patches of palm-fringed sand like Bottom Bay in the southeast.

For more than three centuries Barbados was a British colony and, perhaps unsurprisingly, it retains something of a British feel: the place names, the cricket, horse-racing and polo, Anglican parish churches, and even a hilly district known as Scotland. But the Britishness is often exaggerated, for this is a distinctly West Indian country, covered by a patchwork of sugarcane fields and dotted with tiny rum shops, where calypso is the music of choice, flying fish the favoured food, and cultural influences as likely to emanate from Africa as from Europe.

The people of Barbados, known as Bajans, take great pride in their tiny island of 430 square kilometres and 250,000 people. Literacy is as high as you'll find in any European nation, and Bajans have a deserved reputation for being well-informed and articulate. In writers like George Lamming and calypsonians like the Mighty Gabby the island has produced some of the finest artists in the English-speaking West Indies, while around the world its cricket players – including the great Sir Gary Sobers – have for decades had an influence way out of proportion to the size of their home country.

Tourism of course plays a major part in the country's economy and, in a mature and flourishing democracy, it is obvious that the revenues have been put to good use. The infrastructure is first-rate, with excellent roads, schools and public transport, and there is no sign of the poverty that continues to bedevil some Caribbean islands. Critics of development argue that the island has sold its soul for tourism but, in many ways, Barbados has been a model of how to cope with the new role of tourist mecca suddenly thrust upon many West Indian islands since the 1960s. Development has mostly been pretty discreet, many of the facilities are Bajan-owned, there are no private beaches and no sign of the American fast-food franchises that blight other islands in the region.

Admittedly, there are areas on both the south and west coasts where tourism is utterly dominant and Bajans massively outnumbered by European and American visitors. But, if you want to, it's easy to get away from it. Jump in a bus or a rental car and see the rest of the island: the sugar-growing central parishes, the thinly populated and little-explored north, and the ruggedly beautiful east coast, where you can hike for miles along the beach with only seabirds and the occasional surfer in sight.

When to go

For many visitors, Barbados's tropical climate is its leading attraction – hot and sunny year-round. The weather is at its best during the high season period from mid-December to mid-April, with rainfall low and the heat tempered by cooling trade winds. Things can get noticeably hotter during the summer and, particularly in September and October, the humidity can become oppressive. September is also the most threatening month of the annual hurricane season, which runs officially from June 1 to October 31, though it's worth bearing in mind that, on average, the big blows only hit about once a decade.

As you'd expect, prices and crowds are at their peak during high season, when the main attractions and beaches can get pretty packed. Outside this period everywhere is a little quieter, flight and accommodation prices come down (often dramatically) and you'll find more scope for negotiation on other items.

Barbados's climate

	°F		°C		Rainfall	
	Average daily		Average daily		Average monthly	
	max	min	max	min	in	mm
Jan	83	70	28	21	2.6	66
Feb	83	69	28	21	1.1	28
March	85	70	29	21	1.3	33
April	86	72	30	22	1.4	36
May	87	73	31	23	2.3	58
June	87	74	31	23	4.4	112
July	86	74	30	23	5.8	147
Aug	87	74	31	23	5.8	147
Sept	87	74	31	23	6.7	170
Oct	86	73	30	23	7.0	178
Nov	85	73	29	23	8.1	206
Dec	83	71	28	22	3.8	97

BASICS

GETTING THERE FROM BRITAIN AND IRELAND

Most British and Irish visitors to Barbados are on some form of package tour which includes a charter flight direct to the islands. This is the simplest way of going and, even if you plan to travel independently, a seat on a charter is normally the cheapest too. But charters do have their drawbacks, especially if your plans don't fit into their usual two-week straitjacket. As an alternative, a couple of airlines offer direct scheduled flights from London, and you can find similar fares with other carriers that require a stopover in the USA. There are no direct flights from Ireland to Barbados, but there are good connections via London or, on Aer Lingus or Delta, via New York and Miami (see "Getting There from the USA and Canada", p.7).

Fares, flights and air passes

Most of the discount and specialist travel agents listed opposite can quote fares on scheduled and charter flights, although some (including Campus, STA and USIT which all specialize in youth and student fares) only quote for scheduled flights. Other useful sources of information are the ads in London's *Time Out* magazine and the travel pages in the *Observer* and other Sunday newspapers. *Teletext* and *Ceefax* are also worth a look, as is your local travel agent.

Regardless of where you buy your ticket, fares will depend on the season. Seasonals vary from airline to airline, but mid-December to mid-April is generally classified as **high season**, and the rest of the year **low season**. In July and August, however, mid-priced shoulder season fares come into play.

British Airways fly from London Gatwick from Monday to Saturday and from Heathrow on Saturday and Sunday. BWIA also fly to the island daily. Return fares with both airlines start at between £400 and £500 in low season, reaching £700–800 in high season. It's often cheaper, if less convenient, to change planes in the US, normally in Miami (see p.8). Delta, Virgin, British Airways and American Airlines all fly from London to Miami, with fares as low as £200-250 during the low season.

Charter operators British Caledonian, Britannia and Monarch all fly from London, and Airtours also fly from Manchester. They are normally significantly cheaper than scheduled flights, but tend to arrive and depart at more anti-social hours, and there is little or no flexibility once the ticket is booked. Fares start at as little as £199 during low season, rising to £500+ in high season. Most charter flights are for a fortnight, though you can also find charters for one or three weeks.

Finally, if you fancy flying around more than one Caribbean island, BWIA and the eastern Caribbean airline LIAT offer air passes, available in Britain, which allow you to do just that.

Airlines and discount agents

Airlines
Aer Lingus Dublin ℂ01/844 4777;
Northern Ireland ℂ0645/737747

Air UK Leisure ✆0345/666777
American Airlines ✆0345/789789
British Airways ✆0345/222111
BWIA ✆0181/577 1100
Caledonian ✆01293/56321
Delta Airlines ✆0800/414767; Belfast ✆01232/480526
Virgin Atlantic ✆01293/747747

Discount agents

Budget Travel Dublin ✆01/661 1403
Campus Travel ✆0171/730 8111
Caribbean Travel ✆0181/969 6230
Council Travel ✆0171/437 7767
Flightbookers ✆0171/757 2080
Joe Walsh Tours Dublin ✆01/671 8751; Cork ✆021/277959
The London Flight Centre ✆0171/244 6411
New Look Travel ✆0181/965 8212
Newmont Travel ✆0171/254 6546
Redfern Travel ✆01274/733551
STA Travel ✆0171/361 6262
Trailfinders London ✆0171/938 3366; Dublin ✆01/677 7888
USIT Belfast ✆01232/324073; Dublin ✆01/602 1600

Packages and tours

A **package holiday** can offer excellent value, and often works out much cheaper than arranging separate flights, transfers and accommodation yourself. There are all kinds of deals available, depending on whether you opt for an all-inclusive (hotel room plus all meals), room-only, or self-catering option (usually a hotel room with simple cooking facilities). Most packages are for two weeks, and you may have to shop around to find a one-week or three-week deal.

All-inclusive packages at a three-star hotel start at around £700 per person for a week, £950 for a fortnight, based on double occupancy, while room-only and self-catering deals start at around £450 per peron for a week, £500 for a fortnight, again based on two people sharing. All deals include the flight and transfers from airport to hotel.

A handful of tour operators offer **specialized tours** based, for example, around getting married or catching the West Indies cricket season. And if you want to see Barbados for a day, you could do worse than a Caribbean cruise; these start at around £1000, including a return flight to the embarkation point in Miami (see p.10).

Specialist package and tour operators

Airtours ℂ01706/240033
Calypso Gold ℂ0181/977 9655
Caribtours ℂ0171/581 3517
Cosmos Travel, ℂ0181/464 3444
Hayes and Jarvis ℂ0181/748 008
Joe Walsh Tours Dublin ℂ01/676 3053
Kuoni Travel ℂ01306/742222
Thomas Cook Britain ℂ0990/666222;
Belfast ℂ01232/242341; Dublin ℂ01/677 1721
Thomson Holidays ℂ0171/387 9321
Tropical Places ℂ01342/825123

GETTING THERE FROM THE USA AND CANADA

The most obvious way of getting to Barbados is by air. There are few cheap flights to Barbados, however, and the airlines don't offer special student rates or air passes. Nor does the Caribbean fit too well into a round-the-world (RTW) itinerary. For more leisurely transport, many cruise ships call at the island, and it is even possible to sail there by yacht from Miami.

Fares and flights

Apart from special promotions, the cheapest published fare is usually an **Apex ticket**, although you have to book – and pay – at least 21 days before departure, spend at least seven days abroad, and you tend to get penalized if you change your schedule.

You can normally cut costs further by going through a consolidator or a discount agent, who may also offer **student and youth fares** and a range of other services such as travel insurance, rail passes, car rentals, and tours. Penalties for changing your plans can be stiff, however. Some agents specialize in **charter flights**, which may be cheaper than any scheduled flight, but again departure dates are fixed and withdrawal penalties are high.

Regardless of where you buy your ticket, fares will depend on the season. Definitions vary from airline to airline, but high season generally extends from mid-December to early April and from the end of June to the

7

beginning of September. The rest of the year is considered low season.

The following are typical high/low season APEX fares, departing mid-week, from US/Canadian cities to Grantley Adams Airport in Barbados: NY (US$591/542); Atlanta, same; Chicago (US$765/713); Los Angeles (US$765/713); Miami (US$533/483); Toronto (CAN$900/744).

BWIA flies non-stop out of NY and Miami and offers the lowest fares from these two locations. American Airlines flies non-stop to Barbados from NY and Miami, while Air Jamaica flies out of Los Angeles, Atlanta, Chicago, Baltimore, New York, Newark, Philadelphia, Orlando and Miami. Air Jamaica's fares are slightly better than those of American Airlines, though you have to change planes in Montego Bay, Jamaica.

Another solution is to fly to San Juan, Puerto Rico and then on to Barbados; American Eagle flies to San Juan non-stop from LA, Dallas, Chicago, Baltimore/Washington Dulles, Miami and Kennedy/Newark. Vancouver via New York to San Juan, for example, costs around CAN$697 year round. Flights from Chicago are US$802/542 and from New York US$450/262 in high/low season. From San Juan to Barbados is $150 round-trip, year round, though prices can fluctuate.

BWIA's flight from Toronto, which leaves once a week, is also good value, though Air Canada and Canadian Airlines International offer even lower fares from Montreal and Toronto. Getting from Vancouver to Barbados is a challenge since an overnight stay is ususaly required to catch a flight from the US gateways.

Airlines and discount agents

American Airlines ℭ 1-800/433-7300
American Eagle ℭ 1-800/433-7300

Air Canada ✆1-800/776-3000
Air Jamaica ✆1-800/523-5585
BWIA ✆1-800/538-2942
Canadian Airlines International Canada ✆1-800/665-1177;US ✆1-800/426-7000

Discount agents and consolidators
Council Travel ✆1-800/226-8624
STA Travel ✆1-800/777-0112 or ✆212/627-3111
Travel CUTS ✆1-800/667-2887 Canada only
or ✆416/979-2406
Worldtek Travel ✆1-800/243-1723 or ✆203/772-0470

Packages and tours

Although flights from North America to Barbados can be reasonably priced, you can sometimes find an even less expensive alternative with a **vacation package**. Most cover air fare, transfers, accommodation and airport taxes, and can include meals. Prices start from US$701, leaving from New York or Miami (BWIA Vacations), for seven nights in low season, but generally hover around US$1100 for a two-week stay. Scuba diving and hiking, for example, are activities that are arranged once one has arrived on the island, usually through the hotel.

Tour Operators

Air Jamaica Vacations ✆ 1-800/622-3009
Alken Tours ✆ 1-800/221-6686 or 718/856-7711
BWIA Vacations ✆ 1-800/780-5501 or 718/520-8100
Delta Dream Vacations ✆ 1-800/221-6666 or 954/522-1440
Island Flight Vacations ✆ 1-800/426-4570

GETTING THERE FROM THE USA AND CANADA |

STA Travel ℂ1-800/777-0112 or 212/627-3111
Tour Host International ℂ 1-800/THE HOST or ℂ
212/953-7910
TourScan Inc ℂ 1 800/962 2080 or ℂ 203/655 8091;
www.tourscan.com

By sea

If you plan to **yacht** to Barbados, the US Coast Guard in
Miami will steer you in the right direction (ℂ305/535
4470), or you can call US Sailing (ℂ1 800/-US SAIL 1 or
401/683 0800).

Cruise operators

The fares quoted below are for **low season** (see "By Air")
seven-day cruises in single person/double occupancy
"inside" (no ocean views) cabins, and are exclusive of port
charges which add an extra US$100 to US$130. The cruises
stop only once in Barbados and leave from San Juan, unless
otherwise noted.

Docking in Bridgetown
Carnival Cruise Line ℂ1 800/227 6482; from $519.
Cunard ℂ1 800/221 4770; from $4600. A 116-person lux-
ury "yacht-like" ship that goes from Barbados to Barbados.
Holland American Line ℂ1 800/426 0327 or 206/281
3535; from US$1428 for a **10 day** cruise.
Princess Cruises ℂ 1 800/774 6237; from US$839.
Royal Caribbean International ℂ1 800/327 6700; from
US$699.

Docking in Pricetown
Norwegian Cruise Line ℂ 1 800/327 7030; from
US$839.

GETTING THERE FROM AUSTRALIA AND NEW ZEALAND

Barbados is no bargain destination from Australasia. There are no direct flights from Australia or New Zealand, so you'll have to fly to one of the main US gateway airports and pick up onward connections from there. The least expensive and most straightforward route is via Miami or New York, from where there are frequent flights to Bridgetown.

If you're planning to see Barbados as part of a longer trip, **Round-the-World** (RTW) tickets are worth considering, and are generally better value than a simple return flight. Whatever kind of ticket you're after, first call should be one of the **specialist travel agents** listed below, which can fill you in on all the latest fares and any special offers. If you're a **student** or **under 26**, you may be able to undercut some of the prices given here; STA is a good place to start.

Fares, flights and air passes

All the fares quoted below are for travel during **low or shoulder seasons**, and exclude airport taxes; flying at peak times (primarily Dec to mid-Jan) can add substantially to these prices.

The best fares you're likely to find are the Air New Zealand, United and Qantas regular services to Los Angeles, with connecting flights to Miami flying American Airlines or United: return fares to Miami cost around A\$2259 from the eastern states, rising to A\$2699 from Western Australia. From Miami to Bridgetown, return flights with American Airlines cost A\$350, giving a total return fare in the region of A\$2600–3050. **From New Zealand**, Air New Zealand, Qantas and United fly to Los Angeles, with connections on to Miami. Through fares to Miami start at NZ\$2495; and the return to Bridgetown will add another NZ\$385.

If you plan to indulge in some island-hopping around the Caribbean, BWIA **air passes** can be worthwhile; available for purchase in conjunction with any international carrier, these allow unlimited stopovers within a thirty-day period, and prices start from A\$550/NZ\$590. Passes are valid only within the Caribbean region (including Venezuela and Guyana).

RTW tickets

Given these fares and routings, **round-the-world tickets** that take in **New York or Miami** are worth considering, especially if you have the time to make the most of a few stopovers; see "Getting There from the USA and Canada", p.7, for more on your options for getting to Barbados from New York and Miami.

Ultimately, your choice of route will depend on where else you want to visit besides Barbados, but sample itineraries to whet your appetite: starting from either **Melbourne, Sydney or Brisbane**, flying to Bangkok to Paris to Nice to New York to Los Angeles and then back to Melbourne, Sydney or Brisbane (from A\$1899); or, starting from **Perth**, flying to Los Angeles, New York, Paris and Nairobi before heading back to Perth (from A\$2229).

Airlines

Air New Zealand Auckland ℂ09/357 3000; Sydney ℂ13 2746
American Airlines Sydney ℂ02/9299 3600, toll-free ℂ1800/227 101
BWIA International Airways Sydney ℂ02/9223 7004
Qantas Sydney ℂ13 1211; Auckland ℂ09/357 8900, toll-free 0800/808 767.
United Airlines Sydney ℂ13 1777; Auckland ℂ09/379 3800

Packages and tours

Package holidays from Australia and New Zealand to Barbados are few and far between, and many specialists simply act as **agents** for US-based operators, tagging a return flight from Australasia on to the total cost. **Cruises** account for the largest sector of the market: most depart from Miami, and because prices are based on US dollar amounts, they fluctuate with the exchange rate, but to give some idea, all-inclusive 3-day cruises start from A$650, while 7-day cruises cost upwards of A$1000. The luxury end of the market is also catered for by Caribbean Destinations and Contours, both of which offer **resort**- and **villa-based holidays** as well as cruises, with a choice of accommodation on Barbados – most of it on the west coast of the island. Prices start around A$3500 for 14 days (based on twin-share accommodation and low-season airfares from Australia), and rising inexorably.

None of the adventure-tour operators venture to Barbados; for independent travellers, the cheapest way to visit the Caribbean is as part of a round-the-world or American holiday, making creative use of airpasses – see above.

GETTING THERE FROM AUSTRALIA AND NEW ZEALAND |

Travel Agents

Anywhere Travel Sydney ©02/9663 0411
Brisbane Discount Travel Brisbane ©07/3229 9211
Budget Travel Auckland ©09/366 0061, toll-free
0800/808 040
Destinations Unlimited Auckland ©09/373 4033
Flight Centres Sydney ©13 1600; Auckland ©09/309
6171
Northern Gateway Darwin ©08/8941 1394
STA Travel Australia ©13 1776; fastfare telesales
©1300/360 960; New Zealand ©09/309 0458; fastfare
telesales ©09/366 6673; www.statravelaus.com.au; email:
traveller@statravelaus.com.au
Thomas Cook Australia ©13 1771, direct telesales
©1800/063 913; New Zealand ©09/379 3920
Topdeck Travel Adelaide ©08/8232 7222
Tymtro Travel Sydney ©02/9223 2211 © 1300/652
969

Specialist Agents and Tour Operators

Caribbean Destinations ©1800/816 717
Contours ©03/9329 5211
Creative Tours ©02/9836 2111
Wiltrans ©02/9255 0899

GETTING AROUND

A lot of people come to Barbados, make straight for their hotel and spend the next fortnight lying on the beach. For those who want to tour around and see the island, though, there are are a variety of options.

Though cheap, speedy **buses** and **minibuses** run around the island's coasts and into almost every nook and cranny of the interior, the best way of seeing Barbados is to rent a **car** for a couple of days and cruise around at your own pace – though this isn't cheap. If you just want to make the odd excursion or short trip, it can work out cheaper to hire **taxis**.

By bus

The bus system in Barbados is excellent, with blue government **buses** and yellow, privately owned **minibuses** running all over the island and offering particularly good services up and down the west coast, between Bridgetown and Speightstown, and along the south coast, between Bridgetown and Oistins. The destination is written on a board on the front of the bus and fares are a flat rate B$1.50 – try to have the right change ready. The red and white bus stops are never far apart, and marked "To City" and "Out of City", depending on whether the bus is going towards or away from Bridgetown but, if you're not clear where you're headed, other passengers will invariably help you out.

Privately owned white minivans known as **route taxis**, identified by the ZR on their numberplate, also operate like minibuses, packing in passengers and stopping anywhere en route where they see potential custom. They're

GETTING TO AND FROM THE AIRPORT

Buses run between Grantley Adams International Airport and Bridgetown roughly every half hour (B$1.50), stopping at or near most of the south coast resorts en route. Services to the resorts on the west coast are less frequent. Alternatively, there are numerous **car rental** outlets at the airport, while **taxis** cost around B$40 to the hotels in St James on the west coast, B$50 to Speightstown, B$20 to Crane Bay and B$25 to the resorts in the southwest.

particularly numerous on the south coast and the fare, as on the buses, is B$1.50. Many Bajans don't use route taxis because they consider the drivers to be reckless and totally uninterested in passenger comfort.

By car

Barbados is an easy country to **drive** in; the roads are mostly good and distances are small. Driving is on the left. Rental prices, however, are fairly high, starting at around B$90 per day, B$500 per week, for the mini mokes (opensided buggies) that you'll see all over the island. Third party **insurance** is included in the price; if you don't have a credit card that offers free collision damage insurance, you'll have to pay another B$15–20 per day if you want to cover potential damage to the rental car.

When renting, you'll need a current **licence** from your home country or an international driver's licence and, normally, a **credit card** to make a security deposit. Check the car fully to ensure that every dent, scratch or missing part is inventoried before you set off. When returning the car, don't forget to collect any credit card deposit slip.

The usual suspects – Hertz, Avis et al – no longer operate out of Barbados, and since car-rental companies on the island are all local, it can be easier to organize things once you've arrived. Reliable firms include: Access (✆427 0215), Coconut (✆437 0297), Drive-a-matic (✆422 4000), Hill's (✆426 5280), Jones (✆426 5030), Premier (✆424 2277), Sunny Isle (✆435 7979). Each of these should deliver the car to your hotel.

By taxi

Finding a **taxi** in Barbados – identifiable from a Z on their numberplates – is rarely a problem. Fares are regulated but there are no meters, so agree the fare before you get into the car.

Motorbikes and cycling

Since Barbados is so small, and there are few steep inclines, it would seem like ideal **cycling** territory, yet this mode of transport has never really caught on, and cycle hire is virtually unknown. Hiring a scooter or **motorbike** is easier – prices normally start at around US$30 per day - and can be a fantastic way of touring around, though again you'll need to watch out for drivers on the main roads.

Tours

In case you don't fancy driving, there are various local companies who offer island-wide **sightseeing tours**, either to a set itinerary or customized to your needs.

Remember to check whether the price includes entrance fees to the various attractions. Your hotel may also organize tours direct. If you can't get a good price from any of the companies below, you could check with some of the taxi operators listed in the individual chapters.

Johnson's Stables (©426 5181) can provide a car and driver to take you around for half a day for around B$40 per person (entry fees extra); there's normally a minimum of three to four people, though they'll waive this at quiet times. Boyce's Tours (©425 1103) offer a similar deal, and both companies will be happy to customize an itinerary for you.

Of the more organized tour groups, Chalene Tours (©228 2550) offer a day trip for B$110 per person that visits Speightstown, Farley Hill Park, Bathsheba and Sunbury Plantation House, and includes lunch, drinks and entrance fees, while Island Safari (©432 5337) offer excellent, informative Land-Rover cruises of the island – heading into the wilder places away from the established "sights" – for between B$80 and B$115, including lunch, depending on how much exploring they're doing on a particular day.

EL Scenic Tours (©424 9108) take three daily and well-priced tours: Harrison's Cave for B$50; Harrison's Cave and the Flower Forest for B$80; and Harrison's Cave, the Flower Forest, Bathsheba and St John's Parish Church for B$85. All prices include entrance fees.

Helicopter tours

If you really want to splash out, Bajan Helicopters (©431 0069) offer short but spectacular **helicopter tours** of the island from the heliport in Bridgetown. A twenty-minute ride costs B$145, thirty minutes for B$245.

VISITING OTHER ISLANDS

LIAT (Ⓒ434 5428) runs **flights** to all the nearby islands as well as into Venezuela in South America. Fares start at around B$250 for round-trip flights to St Lucia, St Vincent and Grenada, and most will allow you one or more free stopovers en route. Tickets are sold at a multitude of travel agents island-wide.

If you really want to splash out, a couple of companies offer **day-trips** to the beautiful Grenadine islands, with an early morning flight to Union Island followed by a catamaran trip through several more of the cays, with plenty of snorkelling and a buffet lunch. Prices start at B$490 per person, rising to B$700 if you want to stop off at Mustique for breakfast and a tour of the houses of the rich and famous. Contact Chantours (Ⓒ432 5591) or Grenadine Tours (Ⓒ435 8451).

VISAS AND RED TAPE

Citizens of Britain, Ireland, the US, Canada, Australia and New Zealand can enter Barbados without a visa and stay for up to three months. You will, however, need a passport (valid for at least six months after the date of onward travel) and a return ticket or proof of onward travel. You might also be asked to show that you have sufficient funds to cover your stay; if you can't satisfy the immigration authorities, they have the right to deny you entry.

Embassies and consulates

UK 1 Great Russell Street, London WC1B 3JY, (℃0171/631 4975)
US 800 2nd Avenue, 2nd Floor, New York, NY 10012, ℃212/867-8435; 2144 Wyoming Avenue NW, Washington DC 20008 (℃202/939-9200)
Canada 105 Adelaide St West, Suite 1010, Toronto, Ontario M5H 1P9 (℃ 416/214-9805)
There is no Barbados embassy or consulate in Ireland, Australia or New Zealand

HEALTH AND INSURANCE

If you need medical or dental treatment on the island, you'll find the standard is high, and certainly among the best in the Caribbean. Bridgetown has the 600-bed public Queen Elizabeth Hospital (℃436 6450) and the private Bayview Hospital (℃436 5446), while smaller health centres and clinics are distributed around the island. For an ambulance, call ℃115.

Before buying an insurance policy, check that you're not already covered. Private health plans typically provide some **overseas medical coverage**, although they are unlikely to pick up the full tab in the event of a mishap. Homeowners' or renters' insurance often covers theft or loss of documents, money and valuables while overseas. After exhausting these possibilities, you might want to contact a specialist travel insurance company; your travel agent can usually recommend one (or see p.23).

Health

Travelling in Barbados is usually very safe as far as health is concerned. Food is invariably well and hygienically prepared and the tapwater, drawn from springs and rain filtered by the island's coral, is safe to drink.

No jabs are needed – the major tropical diseases were eradicated long ago – and you'll find that the only real threat to your physical welfare is the intense **Caribbean sun**. Many visitors get badly sunburned on the first day and suffer for the rest of the trip – you'll see them peeling around the island. To avoid their fate, it's advisable to wear a strong sunscreen at all times; if you're after a tan, start strong and gradually reduce the factor. As for exposure times, fifteen minutes a day in the early morning or late afternoon is recommended, if rarely followed; unreconstructed sun-worshippers should at least avoid the heat of the day between 11.30am and 2.30pm. For the sunburned, aloe vera gel is available at the island's pharmacies.

While you're on the beach, steer clear of the **manchineel trees**, recognizable by their shiny green leaves and the small, crab apple-like fruits that will be scattered around. The fruit is poisonous and, when it rains, the bark gives off a poisonous sap which will cause blisters if it drips on you. The sea, too, poses a handful of threats. Don't worry about the rarely seen sharks or barracudas, which won't spoil your visit, but watch out for spiny black **sea urchins**. They're easily missed if you're walking over a patch of sea grass; if you step on one and can't get the spines out, you'll need medical help.

Insurance

Most people will find it essential to take out a good **travel insurance policy** for a trip to Barbados, ideally covering at least medical treatment, theft and loss of baggage. Check first, though, to find out if you already have any coverage: bank and credit cards (particularly American Express) often have certain levels of medical or other insurance included if you use them to pay for your trip; this can be quite comprehensive, anticipating such mishaps as lost or stolen baggage, missed connections and charter companies going bust. Similarly, if you have a good "all risks" home insurance policy, it may well cover your possessions against loss or theft even when overseas, and many private medical schemes also cover you when abroad – make sure you know the procedure and the relevant telephone number. If you're planning a trip to mainland South America, make sure that your insurance extends to the region.

If you plan to participate in **water sports**, you may have to pay an extra premium; check carefully that any insurance policy you are considering will cover you in case of an accident. Note also that very few insurers will arrange on-the-spot payments in the event of a major expense or loss; you will usually be reimbursed only after going home.

In all cases of loss or **theft** of goods, you will have to contact the local police to have a report made out so that your insurer can process the claim; for medical claims, you'll need to provide receipts and supporting bills. If you are going to make a claim, make a note of any time period within which you must lodge it, and keep photocopies of everything you send to the insurer.

British and Irish cover

In Britain and Ireland, travel insurance schemes (from around £35 a month for Barbados) are sold by almost every **travel agent** or **bank**, and by specialist insurance companies. Policies issued by Campus Travel, STA, Endsleigh, Frizzell or Columbus (see below for details) are all good value. Columbus and some banks also do multi-trip policies which offer twelve months' cover for around £90.

North American cover

Premiums for travel to Barbados start at around US$65 for a two-week trip; $85 for three weeks to a month. Longer-term plans are also available. Note that most North American travel policies apply only to items lost, stolen or damaged while in the custody of an identifiable, responsible third party – hotel porter, airline, luggage consignment, etc. Even in these cases, you will have to contact the local police within a certain time limit to have a complete report made out so that your insurer can process the claim.

Australian and New Zealand cover

Travel insurance is available from travel agents or direct from insurance companies (see box). Policies are broadly comparable in premium and coverage; a typical one will cost A$190/NZ$220 for one month.

Travel insurance suppliers

Britain and Ireland
Campus Travel ⓒ0171/730 8111
Columbus Travel Insurance ⓒ0171/375 0011

Endsleigh Insurance ✆0171/436 4451
Frizzell Insurance ✆01202/292333
STA ✆0171/361 6262
USIT Belfast ✆01232/324073; Dublin ✆01/679 8833

USA and Canada

Access America ✆1-800/284-8300
Carefree Travel Insurance ✆1-800/645-2424
Desjardins Travel Insurance (Canada only) ✆1-800/463-7830
ISIS (International Student Insurance Service) – sold by STA Travel ✆1-800/777-0112
Travel Assistance International ✆1-800/821-2828
Travel Guard ✆1-800/826-1300
Travel Insurance Services ✆1-800/937 1387

Australia and New Zealand

AFTA ✆02/9956 4800
Cover More, in Sydney ✆02/9968 1333; elsewhere in Australia toll-free ✆1800/251881
Ready Plan Australia toll-free ✆1800/337462; New Zealand ✆09/379 3399
UTAG, in Sydney ✆02/9819 6855; elsewhere in Australia, toll-free ✆1900/809462

INFORMATION AND MAPS

Before you leave home, it's worth contacting the Barbados Tourism Authority (BTA), if there is one near you. BTA offices stock plenty of information on the country, including brochures on the main tourist attractions and forthcoming events, and a good road map. Once you're in Barbados, you can get the same information from the BTA office at Harbour Road in Bridgetown (©427 2623, fax 426 4080) or from their desk at the airport. Most of the car rental outlets will also provide you with a free map of the island when you rent from them.

Barbados has no detailed listings magazine for music, theatre and cinema, though the free fortnightly magazine *Sunseeker* – available from the tourist office and some hotels – carries details of many of the events. Keep an eye also on the daily papers and on flyers posted up around the island; local radio stations (see p.30) also advertise major events.

BARBADOS ON THE INTERNET

Barbados Tourism Encyclopedia
barbados.org
The official Barbados Tourist Authority Web site – there's a slightly different version at *www.divefree.net/bta.htm*
Calabash Skyviews Caribbean Tourism Hub
www.skyviews.com/barbados

Barbados Tourism Authority overseas

Britain 263 Tottenham Court Rd, London W1P 0LA
(𝄢171 636 9448, fax 171 637 1496)
Canada 105 Adelaide Street West, Suite 1010, Toronto,
Ontario M5H 1P9 (𝄢1 800/268-9122 or 416/214-9880)
Europe Neue Mainzer Strasse 22, D-60311
Frankfurt/Main, Germany (𝄢69 23 23 66, fax 69 23 00 77)
USA 800 Second Avenue, New York NY 10017 (𝄢221-
9831 or 212/986 6516); 3440 Wilshire Boulevard, Suite
1215, Los Angeles CA 90010 (𝄢213/380 2198, fax
213/384 2763)
(The BTA has no branches in Australia or New Zealand)

MONEY AND COSTS

Barbados is not a particularly cheap country to visit,
and prices for many items are at least as much as
you'd pay at home. Negotiation on price is generally
frowned on – taxi rates, for example, are normally
fixed – but, particularly during the off-season of April
to November, it can be worth asking for a reduced
rate for items like accommodation or car rental.

Currency

The island's unit of currency is the **Barbados dollar** (B$),
divided into 100 cents. It comes in bills of B$100, B$50,

B\$20, B\$10, B\$5 and B\$2 and coins of B\$1, B\$0.25, B\$0.10, B\$0.05 and B\$0.01. The rate of exchange is fixed at B\$2 to US\$1 (giving you, at the time of writing, roughly B\$3.2 to UK£1) – though you'll get a fraction less when you exchange money – and the US\$ is usually accepted in payment for goods and services.

Prices are normally quoted in B\$, with the exception of accommodation which is almost universally quoted in US\$, and we have followed this practice in the Guide.

Costs

Apart from the flight, **accommodation** is likely to be the major expense of your trip. Double rooms start at around US\$25, though most of the cheaper options cost around US\$35-40 in winter, US\$30-35 in summer. For something more salubrious, and certainly along the west coast, expect to pay at least US\$70-80 in winter, US\$50-60 in summer. Rooms apart, if you **travel** around by bus and get your **food** from supermarkets and the cheaper cafés, you can just about survive on a **daily budget** of around US\$10-15 per day. Upgrading to one decent meal out, the occasional museum or plantation house visit and a bit of evening entertainment, expect to spend a more realistic US\$25-30; after that, the sky's the limit.

Travellers' cheques and plastic

Easily the safest and most convenient method of carrying money abroad is in the form of **travellers' cheques** and, while sterling and other currencies are perfectly valid and accepted in the island's banks, US dollars travellers' cheques are the best ones to have. They are available for a small commission from most banks, and from branches of American

Express and Thomas Cook; make sure you keep the purchase agreement and a record of cheque serial numbers safe and separate from the cheques themselves. Once in Barbados, they can be cashed at banks (you'll need your passport or other photo ID to validate them) for a small charge.

Major **credit cards** – American Express, Visa, Mastercard – are widely accepted, but don't necessarily expect the smaller hotels and restaurants to take them. You can also use the cards to get cash advances at most banks, though you'll pay both commission to the bank and hefty interest to your credit card company. Royal Bank of Canada has **ATM** machines for those with Visa and Plus system cards, which can be used to withdraw local cash.

Banks and exchange

Banking hours are generally Mon-Thurs 8am–3pm & Fri 8am–5pm; branches of the Caribbean Commercial Bank are also open Sat 9am–noon. Many **hotels** will also exchange money, though if you're changing anything other than US$ the rate is usually a bit worse than the banks.

Emergency cash

If you **run out** of money, you can arrange a telegraphic transfer to most of the banks in Barbados from your home bank account or that of a friend or family member. Bear in mind that such a transfer will attract hefty commission at both ends, so treat this very much as a last resort.

COMMUNICATIONS AND THE MEDIA

Barbados's postal service is extremely efficient. The GPO in Bridgetown is open Mon–Fri 7.30am–5pm and has poste restante facilities for receiving mail. There are also branches across the island, in the larger towns and villages and at the airport (Mon–Fri 8am–3.15pm), and you can buy stamps and send mail at many of the hotels. Postal rates are reasonable: to the USA and Canada, air mail B$0.90, postcards B$0.60; to the UK, air mail B$1.10, postcards $0.70.

Calling within Barbados is simple – most hotels provide a **telephone** in each room and local calls are usually free. You'll also see Bartel **phone booths** all over the island, and these can be used for local and international calls. Most of the booths take phonecards only – they're available at hotels, post offices and some shops and supermarkets. For finding numbers, hotel rooms and phonebooths often have a directory; failing that, call directory assistance on ©119. To make a collect call, dial ©01, plus the area code (minus the first 0) and number you wish to reach.

Press and radio

As always, local newspapers and radio are a great way to find out what's on the nation's mind. The two daily papers, the *Advocate* and the *Nation*, concentrate on domestic news, though there is a token gesture towards international news and, invariably, a big sports section. The radio stations are the public service channel **Voice of Barbados** (95.3 FM), and the commercial **CBC** (100.1 FM). They both carry news, sport, chat shows and music, mostly international hits with a sprinkling of Bajan tunes. The most entertaining show is Voice of Barbados's lively and outspoken phone-in *Down to Brass Tacks*, which goes out every day at 11.30am.

INTERNATIONAL CALLS

PHONING BARBADOS FROM ABROAD

Dial your international access code (see below)
+ 246 + seven digit number

UK ℂ001   USA ℂ011   Canada ℂ011
Australia ℂ0011   New Zealand ℂ00

PHONING ABROAD FROM BARBADOS

Dial country code (see below)
+ area code minus first 0 + number

UK ℂ011 44   USA ℂ1   Canada ℂ1
Australia ℂ61   New Zealand ℂ64

FESTIVALS, EVENTS AND PUBLIC HOLIDAYS

The main festival in Barbados is the summertime Crop Over (see p.171), which reaches its climax in Kadooment Day when the festival monarchs are crowned. There are plenty of other events to distract you from the beach as well, including international cricket and windsurfing tournaments, a jazz festival, a small literary Festival of Creative Arts, and and even a festival devoted to fish. The local and overseas tourist boards (see p.26) have full details of all the activities – alternatively, call the appropriate number in the box.

ANNUAL EVENTS

Jan	**Barbados Jazz Festival** ℭ429 2084
	Barbados Windsurfing Championships ℭ426 5837
	Red Stripe Cricket Competition ℭ426 5128
Feb	**Holetown Festival** ℭ430 7300
March	**Holder's opera season** (see p.80)
	Test cricket ℭ426 5128
	Oistins Fish Festival ℭ428 6738 (see p.66)
April	**Congaline Street Festival** ℭ424 0909 (see p.171)
May	**Gospelfest** ℭ430 7300
July–Aug	**Crop Over Festival** (see p.171)
Oct	**Barbados International Triathlon** ℭ435 7000
Nov	**Caribbean Surfing Championship** ℭ435 6377
	Festival of Creative Arts ℭ424 0909
Dec	**Barbados Road Race Series**

PUBLIC HOLIDAYS

New Year's Day	Jan 1
Errol Barrow Day	Jan 21
Good Friday	
Easter Monday	
Labour Day	May 1
Whit Monday	eighth Mon after Easter
Kadooment Day	first Mon in Aug
United Nations Day	first Mon in Oct
Independence Day	Nov 30
Christmas Day	Dec 25
Boxing Day	Dec 26

SHOPPING

If you want to take home something authentically Bajan, check out the craft stalls at Pelican Village and Temple Yard in Bridgetown (see p.47), or wait for them to find you – vendors on the most popular beaches, particularly Accra Beach on the south coast, regularly set up stands selling clothing, carved wooden figurines and Haitian-style paintings of markets and other traditional scenes. The Best of Barbados gift shops dotted around the island also sell decent quality souvenirs, from books and prints to T-shirts and rum – perhaps the most authentically Bajan souvenir of all (see p.49).

Other than that, you're largely restricted to the familiar **duty-free** options, with a massive array in Broad Street in Bridgetown (see p.46). If you're after duty-free liquor, jewellery, clothes, cameras or perfume, you'll find all the shops you need there (Mon–Fri 8.30am–4.30pm Sat 8.30am–1pm). Take your passport or air ticket as proof of visitor status.

DRUGS, TROUBLE AND HARASSMENT

Compared to what you'll encounter in Jamaica or several other Caribbean islands, harassment in Barbados is extremely mild. Nevertheless, the hassle can be a pain, particularly around St Lawrence Gap – where you'll invariably be offered drugs or pressed to look at some uninspiring crafts – and at some of the less-visited beauty spots like Cove Bay in the north, where a few guys will ask your name, introduce themselves, then try to sell themselves as (quite unneeded) guides. Just be firm in saying no thanks and they'll leave you alone. The same is true of the _Divi_ resort timeshare sellers, set up in stalls

around the island, who pester you to visit the resort – where you'll be given lunch in return for a couple of hours of hard sell – so that they can claim a commission.

Police ℂ112   Fire ℂ113   Ambulance ℂ115

Violent crime involving tourists is rare but not unheard of. After dark, it's advisable to steer clear of unlit or unpatrolled areas of the beach, and you'll probably want to avoid the rougher areas of Bridgetown (see p.38). **Drugs** present an increasing problem on the island, particularly a growing use of crack cocaine, which is leading to a rise in theft and burglary to finance the habit. Marijuana use is just as widespread – and equally illegal – and often distributed on the beaches, particularly on the south coast, to likely-looking punters. If you want it, you can get it, but bear in mind that there are plenty of undercover police around, and daily stories in the local press of tourists facing heavy fines for possession.

DRUGS, TROUBLE AND HARASSMENT

THE GUIDE

BRIDGETOWN AND AROUND

With a gorgeous location beside the white sand beaches of Carlisle Bay, busy, modern **Bridgetown** is the capital and only city of Barbados. One of the oldest cities in the Caribbean, founded in 1628 by a tiny group of British settlers, it is home to around 40 percent of the island's population (some 100,000 people). The town is situated around an inlet, carved by the Caribbean Sea, which became known as the Careenage. The early settlers, finding an Amerindian wooden bridge across the water, named the area Indian River Bridge, from which the present name eventually derived.

Despite its proximity to a mosquito-infested swamp, the settlement expanded rapidly; an early historian described it as "a city so ill situate, for if they had considered health, as they did convenience, they would never have set it there". But Carlisle Bay offered a safe harbour, and from the seventeenth century onwards the trade in sugar and slaves brought fortunes to the town's merchants, who built their increasingly grand warehouses along the waterfront. Most of the great buildings of these "golden years", however, were swept away in a series of destructive fires and hurricanes; only a handful predate the last great fire of 1860. The architecture of Bridgetown today is largely a blend of attractive, balconied colonial buildings, warehouses and brash modern office blocks.

The centre of activity is the Careenage, parking place for numerous sleek yachts overlooked by the **Barbadian parliament** and a rather forlorn and out-of-place statue of Admiral Nelson. A number of the island's main religious buildings are within five minutes' walk of here, including **St Michael's Cathedral** and the Jewish **synagogue**, both erected on the sites of their mid-seventeenth century originals.

Just north of the city there are a couple of **rum factories** that you can tour (you'll usually be given a snifter or two to enhance the visit), while **Tyrol Cot** is an unusual nineteenth-century house that was home to two of the island's leading post-war politicians, Sir Grantley Adams and his son Tom Adams.

Southeast is the historic **Garrison Savannah**, where the British empire maintained its Caribbean military headquarters from 1780 to 1905. It's an evocative place; the huge grassy savannah, today a racecourse and public park, was once the army's parade ground. The ranks of brightly coloured buildings around its edge were all used for military purposes; a couple of them now house the **Barbados Museum** and the **Barbados Gallery of Art**, both of which deserve a visit if you've any interest in the island's history and culture.

Bridgetown is an extremely **safe** city, even at night, though you may want to avoid the seedy area southeast of the Fairchild Street bus station, particularly around Nelson Street and Jordan's Lane where the city's red light district is located.

Getting there and getting around

Fast, efficient **buses and minibuses** run to the city from points all over the island. If you're coming from the south coast, these pass the garrison area before terminating beside the Fairchild Street bus station. Coming from the west coast, most make their final stop at the corner of Tudor and James Streets – if you're heading to the Garrison you'll want to pick up a bus marked "Oistins", which bypasses the city centre, or head into the centre and take a second bus from Fairchild Street. If you're driving into Bridgetown, you'll have to negotiate a slightly tricky one-way system, but there are plenty of safe, inexpensive areas to park right in the town centre. Once you're there, the easiest way to see the sights of central Bridgetown is **on foot**.

Information

The main office of the **Barbados Tourism Authority** (Mon–Fri 8.30am–4.30pm) on Harbour Street is crammed with brochures and leaflets on hotels, restaurants and attractions, as well as the free *Visitor* and *Sunseeker* magazines, which carry listings of what's on in the forthcoming weeks. Big events, from live stage shows to international cricket matches, are also announced on the radio and on **flyers** posted around town.

For details of accommodation in Bridgetown, see p.128.

The city

A good place to start your tour of Bridgetown is beside the **Careenage**, a long, thin finger of water that pushes right into the city centre. As a protected spot, free from ocean swells, this is where British trading ships were traditionally brought for "careening" – hoisting onto their sides to have their hulls scraped clean of barnacles and slapped with a new coat of paint – as they awaited loading up with barrels of sugar and rum to take back to Europe. Today, the Careenage continues to offer a relatively safe refuge during storms and hurricanes, and you'll always find plenty of expensive yachts and fishing boats moored at its western end. Parliament, smart restaurants, busy shopping streets and the city's main nightclub can all be found in the immediate vicinity, some of them housed in old, restored warehouses.

Two bridges cross the Careenage, linking north and south Bridgetown as they have for centuries, though the old, rickety wooden bridges have now been replaced in more durable concrete. Nearest the sea, the **Chamberlain Bridge** commemorates British Colonial Secretary Joseph Chamberlain's role in securing financial aid for the island's sugar industry in 1900. In front of the bridge stands the **Independence Arch** – erected in 1987 to celebrate the twenty-first birthday of Barbadian independence – which carries the national flag, motto and pledge of allegiance. A stone's throw away, the **Charles Duncan O'Neal Bridge** remembers the man who founded the country's first political party, the Democratic League, in 1924. Just to the east, **Fairchild Street** holds the island's main bus terminal and, beyond it, a huge **public market**, piled high with yams, breadfruit, mangoes and bananas.

For more about the life and career of Charles Duncan O'Neal, see p.196.

TRAFALGAR SQUARE

Map 3, F5.

On the north side of the Chamberlain bridge, a bronze **statue** of the British Admiral Horatio Nelson stands in tiny **Trafalgar Square**, surrounded by the whirlwind of Bridgetown traffic. In the early nineteenth century, with Napoleon's forces on the rampage around the world, Barbados – like all the British West Indian islands – was under threat from France's strong Caribbean-based navy. Nelson, commanding a British fleet in pursuit of the French, stopped briefly on the island in June 1805, just four months before he was killed at the Battle of Trafalgar. In gratitude, the Barbadian parliament granted funds for a statue by the British sculptor Richard Westmacott, which was erected in 1813. If you've seen Nelson's Column in London's Trafalgar Square (also designed by Westmacott, seventeen years later), the statue here seems rather small and incongruous, and it's hard to disagree with the lyrics of *Take Down Nelson* – a big hit for local calypsonian Mighty Gabby – that it might be more appropriate to "put up a Bajan man" in his place.

THE PARLIAMENT BUILDINGS

Map 3, F4. Open during parliamentary sessions only

Nelson faces east, towards an **obelisk** commemorating the Barbadians who died in World War I, behind which the tiny, well-kept **Fountain Gardens** are home to an ornamental fountain, put up in 1865, shortly after piped water was first introduced to the capital. Across the road from the fountain, the **Parliament Buildings** hold the island's two houses of parliament, the assembly and the senate. Barbados's parliament, established in 1639, is one of the oldest in the world. In its early years it met in a series of taverns and private homes, before moving to the eighteenth-century building that now houses the High Court (see p.44). The present neo-Gothic buildings, put up in the 1870s, surround an arcaded courtyard. A churchy clock tower completes the ensemble. If you're in town while parliament is meeting you are free to watch from the public gallery provided you're properly dressed (no shorts). Inside the debating chamber, on the upper floor of the east wing, a series of stained glass windows depict thirteen British sovereigns, starting with James I and including Oliver Cromwell and a very young Queen Victoria.

ST MICHAEL'S CATHEDRAL

Map 3, H3. Daily 9am–4pm; free

About 200m east of parliament along St Michael's Row, the large, red-roofed **St Michael's Cathedral** is the country's principal Anglican place of worship. A stone church was first erected here in 1665, although the present building mostly dates from 1786 and was consecrated as a cathedral in 1825, when Barbados got its first bishop. It's a spacious, airy place, with a large barrel roof, and incorporates some fine mahogany carving in the pulpit and choir. The walls are decorated with a series of monumental sculptures, most notably the relief in the choir dedicated to the city's first bishop, William Hart Coleridge, while the Lady Chapel, added in 1938 at the eastern end, is splashed with colour from its stained glass. The cathedral's sprawling churchyard is the resting-place for many of the island's most prominent figures, including first premier Sir Grantley Adams and his son Tom Adams; if you're there in spring you may be lucky enough to catch it with the red frangipani trees in full bloom.

QUEEN'S PARK HOUSE

Map 3, I3. Daily 10am–1pm & 2–6pm; free

The striking building that towers up behind St Michael's Cathedral is the island's **Central Bank**, at eleven stories the tallest edifice in Barbados; it also holds the country's main concert venue, the Frank Collymore Hall. Continuing east, five minutes' walk brings you to **Queen's Park**, a large open space that's a combination of public park and sports pitches. The main feature of the park is the classically Georgian **Queen's Park House**, built in 1783 as a residence for the general commanding the British armed forces in this part of the Caribbean, and continuing in that role until the British garrison left the island in 1905. Today the house serves as an art gallery, showing changing exhibitions of mostly local art, and as an occasional theatre. It's a laid-back place, and there are always plenty of people around, hanging out or just catching some shade, and there's also a small snack bar. In front of the house is a colossal and ancient baobob tree, eighteen metres in circumference.

THE OLD CITY

Back in the town centre, a network of narrow lanes link the main roads above the parliament buildings, marking the first parts of the city to have been developed. Bridgetown's oldest surviving building is probably the attorneys' office, **Harford Chambers**, on the corner of Lucas and James Streets, with its irregular brickwork and classic Dutch gables characteristic of the city's seventeenth-century architectural style. Immediately opposite, the **Aswad Man Shop**, with its cast-iron first floor balcony projecting over the pavement, dates from around 1840.

Heading north up Coleridge Street takes you past the gleaming white police station and the adjacent **High Court**, built in 1730 and originally home to the city's parliament, prison and courts – law-makers, -breakers and -enforcers all on the same premises. The politicians and prisoners have since moved elsewhere, leaving the lawyers in sole charge. The imposing building next door is the city's **public library** (Mon–Sat 9am–5pm), with the words "Free Library" proudly embossed above the grand, columned entrance. The Barbados parliament passed an act providing for a free library service in 1847, three years before Britain established the same facility, though this building – paid for by American philanthropist Andrew Carnegie – was only opened in 1904.

Across the road from the library, the elaborate **drinking fountain** was a gift to the city from John Montefiore, one of its leading Jewish traders, in 1865. Though not as jauntily painted as in its heyday, the fountain still has stone reliefs of Prudence, Justice, Fortitude and Temperance and imprecations to the thirsty citizens of Bridgetown to "Be sober minded" and "Look to the end".

The synagogue

Map 3, E1. Daily 10am–4pm; free

Across the road from the fountain, the pink and white

synagogue was first built in 1655 and rebuilt after hurricane damage in 1833. Jews were among the earliest settlers in Barbados; many of them arrived in the 1650s to escape the Inquisition in Brazil, bringing a knowledge of sugar-cane cultivation that was to prove crucial in boosting the island's fledgling agriculture. In 1681 there were around 260 Jews on the island – almost five percent of the population – many of them establishing successful shops and other businesses in the area around the synagogue, on roads like Swan Street (once known as Jew Street).

By around 1900, though, a long-term decline in the sugar industry had led many of the business class to emigrate, and the country's Jewish population had shrunk to fewer than twenty people. In 1929, its congregation reduced to just one person, the synagogue was sold to a private buyer and converted into offices, and in 1983 the government acquired it by compulsory purchase, planning to demolish it and build a new Supreme Court on the site.

However, a revitalized Jewish community – boosted during the 1930s and 1940s by refugees from Europe – persuaded the government to let them take the building back, and, with financial aid from Jewish groups overseas, extensive restoration has returned it to something like its original shape. The interior has been attractively restored, with replicas of the original glass chandeliers and a few authentic relics, including some cedarwood pews from 1834 and an old alms box. A series of newspaper articles displayed on the walls describes the restoration work and recounts some of the history. Outside, the Jewish cemetery is one of the oldest in the Western hemisphere, with dozens of cracked tombstones – some of them dating back to the seventeenth century – inscribed in Hebrew, English and (a relic of the settlers from Brazil) Portuguese.

THE SYNAGOGUE |

BROAD STREET AND CHEAPSIDE

Much of central Bridgetown is given over to shopping, with dozens of duty-free stores lined up to compete for the cruise-ship dollar. The main drag is **Broad Street** – a duty-free paradise that runs northwest from Trafalgar Square. This has been the city's market centre since the mid-seventeenth century, and still retains some splendid colonial buildings amid the modern chaos of clothes shops, jewellery stores, fast food joints and fruit vendors. It's worth a stroll, even if you're not planning to shop.

If you want to take advantage of duty-free shopping opportunities, remember to carry your passport and airline ticket.

Halfway along, the enormous, late nineteenth-century **Mutual Life Building**, with its twin silver-domed towers and exquisite cast-iron fretwork, is the most striking of Bridgetown's colonial-era buildings.

St Mary's Church

Map 3, B3.

Further along, on the right, is red-roofed **St Mary's Church**. Built in 1827 on the site of the city's first church, it's a splendid piece of Georgian Neoclassicism, apart from the turreted tower which was tacked on several decades later. Sadly, the church is often locked, but it's worth checking out the jalousied south porch and the shady graveyard where many Bajan luminaries are buried, including Samuel Jackson Prescod who was, in

1843, the first non-white elected for the national parliament.

Temple Yard and Pelican Village

Beyond St Mary's Church, Broad Street runs into **Cheapside**, where you'll find the station for buses and minibuses heading north, as well as the General Post Office and one of the city's larger public markets. On your left, Temple Street runs down to the waterfront past a row of wooden stalls that mark the edge of **Temple Yard**, where many of the city's Rastas have set up small businesses selling sandals and other hand-crafted leather goods, as well as their distinctive red, gold and green jewellery and headgear. The area takes its name from an early nineteenth-century masonic lodge, or temple, used by the Order of the Ancient Masons, but destroyed in the 1831 hurricane.

Below here, **Pelican Village** on Harbour Street is a shopping complex built on reclaimed land, with a small art gallery, a dozen or so stores selling batiks, T-shirts and other souvenirs, and a couple of snack bars.

Kensington Oval

Map 2, B8. Daily 9am–4pm

Back on Cheapside, Fontabelle – at the far end of the street – runs northwest towards the city's shallow harbour, where the tour boats and Atlantis submarine are berthed (see p.176). Just before you reach the top of Fontabelle, a right turn leads to the **Kensington Oval**, the island's premier cricket ground and venue for international test matches.

Cricket devotees will want to take a look around, even if there is no game in progress. For the best view of the ground, you can climb the 3Ws stand – named after the island's three master batsmen of the 1940s and 50s, Sir Frank Worrell, Everton Weekes and Sir Clyde Walcott – or the Sir Garfield Sobers stand, named after the greatest cricketing all-rounder the world has known. A small gift shop sells cricket souvenirs, including West Indies caps and videos. For information on forthcoming games and ticket availability, call ✆436 1397.

For more on the Bajan passion for cricket, see p.201.

North of the City

Just above Kensington Oval, the Spring Garden Highway heads north along the west coast (see Chapter Three), skirting the beach almost all the way to historic Speightstown in the far northwest (see p.87). Much of the area immediately north of Bridgetown is given over to industrial production, including a couple of **rum factories** that are open for tours. To the northeast is **Tyrol Cot**, the former home of the island's first premier, Sir Grantley Adams.

Mount Gay Rum Factory

Map 2, B8. Mon–Fri 9am–4pm, 45min tours every half hour; B$10. The **Mount Gay Rum Factory**, just north of town on the Spring Garden Highway, offers marginally the better of the two tours. This starts with a short film giving the history of the company, which first distilled rum on the island in 1703 and is reckoned to be the world's oldest surviving pro-

The story of rum

Rum has been a key part of Barbadian life for over three centuries, and you couldn't choose a better place to acquire a taste for the stuff. Famous as the drink of pirates and as "grog", dished out to sailors in the British navy to keep them from mutiny, it's the most potent by-product of the sugar that's been grown all over the island since the 1640s. And though production is now mechanized, the basic method hasn't changed much over the centuries.

It takes around ten to twelve tonnes of sugar cane to produce just half a bottle of rum. The juice is extracted, boiled and put through a centrifuge, producing thick, sticky molasses. This is then diluted with water, and yeast is added to get the stuff fermenting. After fermentation, it's heated at the distillery, where the evaporating alcohol is caught in tanks.

In rum-shops across the island, small knots of men (and occasionally women) prop up the bar beside a bottle of cheap white rum and a bottle of water, mixed to the desired strength. The choice of drink is a fine art, with a variety of bottle sizes – miniature, mini, flask, quart and pint in ascending order of size – and an equally varied selection of rums. White rum is also the basis of most rum cocktails, although there are several richer, mellower options, from the golden rums of *Cockspur* and *Mount Gay* to the latter's fabulous *Extra Old* dark rum, best drunk neat over ice. Their darker colour is acquired from the charred American oak barrels in which they are left to mature.

ducer of the stuff. *Mount Gay* rum is actually distilled at the company's factory in St Lucy, but the tour shows you all the later stages in the production process, including refining, ageing, blending and bottling.

The highlight is probably the vast, cool storage area, crammed with barrels oozing the sweet, heady smell of rum, where the "angel's share" of evaporated rum drips from the ceiling. After you've finished snooping around, you can head to the bar, where the barman demonstrates how to be a rum-taster, and you're given a complimentary cocktail – sit outside and sip it on the verandah overlooking the attractively landscaped gardens. There's also a small shop selling the distillery's products (although you'll find them cheaper at the duty-free shops in town) and assorted T-shirts and other paraphernalia.

Malibu Visitor Centre

Map 2, B8. Mon–Fri 9–11am & noon–4pm, tours every 30 min; B$10.

The second rum tour is at the **Malibu Visitor Centre**, adjoining the West India Rum Distillery three minutes' drive further up the highway and signposted on your left as you head away from town. All of the world-famous *Malibu* coconut-flavoured white rum (and the less well-known lime-flavoured stuff) is manufactured here, and you get pretty much the same tour as at Mount Gay. The factory is right on the edge of the sea – the visitor centre even has its own little beach, where you can chill out with a complimentary cocktail once you've finished your tour – and you get a beautiful view of the turquoise sea as you explore the distilling tanks on the upper deck of the building.

TYROL COT

Map 2, B7. Mon–Fri 9am–5pm; B$10.

Five minutes' drive northeast of Bridgetown's busy new

port, the exquisite little house at **Tyrol Cot** was the launch pad for two of the island's most illustrious political careers. From 1929 it served as the home of Sir Grantley Adams, the first elected leader of pre-independence Barbados, and it was the birthplace of his son, Tom Adams, the nation's prime minister from 1976 until his death in 1985. The building itself has some unusual architectural features, while the family's memorabilia scattered around the place offer some glimpses into mid-century political life on the island.

The single-storey, coral block house was built in 1854 by William Farnum, one of the island's leading architects, and combines classic European and vernacular Caribbean styles. The Demerera windows, for example, are framed by Roman arches but contain adjustable double-jalousied shutters, with sloping slats which keep out rain and sun but let in light and allow air to circulate. Each of the windows also has a small but intricate cast-iron guard at its base, a flamboyant if rather eccentric addition. Inside, a collection of the family's furniture includes an ancient short-wave radio, used for tuning into the latest news and cricket scores from the BBC World Service, various mahogany antiques and Sir Grantley's personal stuff – law books, photos of obscure Greek ruins and the flag of his political dream, the Federation of the West Indies, of which he was the first and only prime minister.

For more on Sir Grantley and Tom Adams, see p.197.

Outside the house, a tiny **heritage village** has been built, featuring half a dozen old-fashioned chattel houses built to a variety of designs. Several of the houses showcase traditional handifcrafts, with local potters, artists and basket-

TYROL COT

makers selling (and occasionally demonstrating) their crafts, and there's a typical Barbadian rum-shop where you can get a drink and a bite to eat.

The Garrison Area

By the late seventeenth century, sugar-rich Barbados had become one of the most important of Britain's overseas possessions. Amid continual strife with France and Holland, the British decided to make sure its West Indian colony was heavily fortified against invasion. The most vulnerable part of the island was its calm west coast, and defensive forts were erected along its length, with the biggest of them – Charles Fort (see p.57) – protecting Carlisle Bay and the capital, Bridgetown. In 1705, work was begun on a major land fort nearby, known as St Ann's Fort and designed to offer back-up protection, with thick ramparts, large store-rooms, powder magazines and a well-stocked armoury. By 1780, as Barbados developed, the British decided to make the island the regional centre for their West Indian troops, and more and more army buildings were put up around the fort.

Today, this part of the city's outer zone, just a couple of kilometres south of the centre, is known as the **Garrison area**. Chock full of superb Georgian architecture, it remains one of Bridgetown's most evocative and attractive districts. It retains the most attractive of the island's colonial **military buildings** including, in a restored jail, the **Barbados Museum**. A short walk from the museum, the **National Art Gallery** merits a quick visit while, just south of here on Needham's Point, the **military cemetery** lies beside the modern *Hilton Hotel* and its attractive beach.

THE SAVANNAH

The centre of the Garrison area is the **Savannah**, a huge grassy space that served as the army's parade ground. The military buildings – barracks, quartermaster's store and hospitals, as well as the fort itself – stand in a rough square around its outer edges, flanked by coconut palms and large mango trees. The savannah is still almost permanently active, with sports grounds and play areas bounded by the city's **race track**, which sees action several times a year, particularly during the island's Gold Cup horse race, held in March, when the stands to the north are packed with racegoers. On Independence Day, November 30, the island's forces – the Coast Guard, the Barbados Defence Force, and the younger cadets – maintain tradition by parading on the savannah in front of the island's governor-general.

Of the old military buildings that dot the edges of the savannah, many have been renovated and are now put to other use. To the south, you can still see the thick eighteenth-century walls of **St Ann's Fort** (now used by the Barbadian defence force and closed to visitors) while, just north of here, the spectacular **Main Guard** – with its tall, bright red tower and green cupola – is the area's most striking construction. This was the guardhouse, built in 1803, where court-martials and subsequent punishments were carried out, and you're normally free to wander around the building, though there's little to see. Outside, ranks of ancient but well-preserved black iron cannons point menacingly across the savannah towards some superbly restored **barracks buildings**, which now serve as government offices. Each has a grand double staircase, a long upstairs gallery and, below, an elegant arcade fronted by a row of Roman arches.

The Barbados Museum

Map 2, B8. Mon–Sat 9am–5pm, Sun 2–6pm; B$10.

Housed in the Garrison's old military prison on the east side of the savannah, the **Barbados Museum** is a treat. The entrance is flanked by rows of palms and a couple of ancient cannons. Inside, a series of galleries run clockwise around an airy central courtyard that used to ring with the sound of prisoners breaking stones. The place is stuffed with interesting exhibits and informative displays on the island's history and culture. Don't try to rush it – there's a lot to see and a good little café for when you want to take a break. Once a week the courtyard is the venue for *1627 and All That*, an evening of dance and story-telling (see p.165), and your entry fee includes a chance to tour the museum.

The museum's first gallery focuses on **flora and fauna**, opening with small exhibitions on the country's reefs, shells, birds and green monkeys, then moves into the **history and prehistory** section. This is one of the museum's strong points, with exhibits on the Amerindians – the first inhabitants of Barbados – and the country's evolution from a sugar-based slave society through emancipation and the early struggles of the majority black population to today's democratic, independent nation. The Amerindian finds include some immaculate little shell carvings of human figures, dating from 1000 to 1500 AD, while the more modern sections include cowrie shells from an eighteenth-century slave burial, probably brought from West Africa where they served as currency, and a rare seventeenth-century Bellarmine jug bearing a caricature of an unpopular Italian cardinal.

For more on the history of Barbados and the struggle for emancipation, see p.189.

Don't miss the small gallery at the far end of the history rooms, on the right. This holds a dozen or so **historic maps** of the island, showing how it has changed and developed since 1657. There's also a great little section on the history of the chattel house – the colourful box houses that you'll see all over Barbados. Across the courtyard from here are three **period rooms**, showing what a typical bedroom, living-room and dining-room would have looked like in one of the plantation houses. Opposite, there is a gallery of **prints and paintings** of old Barbados, with a spectacular shell plate in the middle of the floor. Alongside are a gallery devoted to the island's **military history** – including part of a German U-boat that ended up in Carlisle Bay in 1942 – and a tiny room that was once a **prisoner's cell** in the old jail.

The next galleries include a room of **African crafts**, including traditional masks and musical instruments from all over the continent, and another given over to **decorative arts** from all over the world, with glassware from England, including some fabulous and unusual Bristol blue glass, eighteenth-century ceramics from China, Greek and Russian religious icons and some exquisite scrimshaw – pieces of ivory, bone and shell carved by sailors to while away their days at sea. Finally, there is a **temporary exhibition gallery**, often given over to the work of top local artists, and you'll have a chance to buy postcards, books and souvenirs from the museum's **gift-shop**.

THE BARBADOS MUSEUM

The Barbados Gallery of Art

Map 2, B8. Tues–Sat 10am–5pm; B$5.

Opened with a flourish in late 1996, the tiny **Barbados Gallery of Art**, directly across the Garrison Savannah from the National Museum, is devoted to art of the island and from the wider Caribbean. The first room showcases the permanent collection – winners of the annual national art exhibition, plus "audience favourites" from among the other entries. For a room with only nine pieces of art, there is considerable variation in subject-matter and style, from the naturalistic blue and green landscape of Wayne Branch's *Bethesda* to the fabulously colourful *Caribbean Woman As Embrace*, by Annalee Davis, with its chain of smiley, happy people and jumbled emblems from the island's past and present – flying fish, the flag, slave chains and a plantation house. The central sculpture, *King Dyal* by John Flavius – a nattily dressed old man with a green bicycle and a white stick – depicts a real Bajan character who, until his recent and much-lamented death, was seen similarly attired at every national event, from test matches to music festivals. There's only one other room, which holds temporary exhibitions from the gallery's collection – anything from charcoal portraits of leading Bajan personalities to landscapes from around the island – or travelling exhibitions of works from Cuba, Haiti or other West Indian islands.

NEEDHAM'S POINT

Map 2, B8.

Heading back briefly towards town, a left turn takes you out through **Aquatic Gap** – home to several expensive hotels and restaurants – including the all-inclusive *Island Inn Hotel*, housed in an old army rum store (see p.130) – to the tiny peninsula of **Needham's Point**. One of the earliest British colonial forts, **Fort Charles**, was built here during the 1660s and, though it fell into ruin long ago, parts of the old walls have been incorporated into the grounds of the sprawling *Hilton Hotel*, which (together with a large oil refinery) dominates the peninsula and overlooks a pleasant, bustling white sand beach, that is popular with families from the city at weekends. Unknown to most of the guests, the hotel also sits astride the old military burial ground, though a new **military cemetery** (daily; free) was established in 1820 on land nearby. Old tombs in the small grassy compound recall British troops and their families who died on duty in the colony; more modern memorials are testament to Barbadians who served the Allied war effort during the two world wars.

THE SOUTH COAST

The southwestern parish of **Christ Church** was the birthplace of tourism in Barbados, and is still dominated by the trappings of the holiday industry. The main highway hugs the coast, linking a string of small resorts; each consists of a fringe of white sand beach backed by a cluster of hotels, restaurants and tourist facilities. On the whole, the area is not as beautiful as the west coast, nor as dominated by the staggering palaces of the mega-rich, but the beaches are just as fine, there are plenty of good restaurants and prices are much more reasonable.

As you head east from Bridgetown towards the airport, several of the coastal towns bear the names (and some of the atmosphere) of British seaside resorts. Each has its speciality, however: you'll find the best beaches at **Rockley** and **Worthing**, the liveliest restaurants and nightlife at **St Lawrence Gap**, and a bustling local scene at **Oistins**, while the quieter beaches at **Silver Sands** attract windsurfers and those who want to spend their holiday strolling on relatively deserted stretches of sand.

On the other side of the airport, in the southeast of the island, you enter the far less developed parish of **St Philip**. There's just a handful of hotels here, but the scenery is spectacular, with the Atlantic waves lashing the rocky coast for most of the year. **Sam Lord's Castle** – more grand mansion than castle – is worth a look if you're in the area, while nearby **Bottom Bay** is one of the prettiest beaches in Barbados. Just inland, **Sunbury Great House**, recently rebuilt on the site of a centuries-old sugar plantation, offers a glimpse of traditional life on the island, and there's a small zoo nearby at **Oughterson Great House**.

Getting around

Getting around the south coast is a breeze. Buses and minibuses run from Bridgetown as far as Sam Lord's Castle, passing through most of the tourist zones on the coast, while route taxis go as far as Silver Sands. Service stops around midnight, so you'll need a car or a private taxi after that. Getting here from the west coast is a little harder – buses run between Speightstown and Oistins, usually bypassing Bridgetown, though they're less frequent than the ones that ply the south coast. If you're driving, Highway 7 runs along the coast between Bridgetown and Oistins, from where it doglegs up past the airport and on to Crane Bay and Sam Lord's Castle.

**For details of accommodation, on the south coast,
see p.130; for eating and drinking see p.148.**

Christ Church

Most of the island's "lower end" tourism is concentrated in the southwest of Barbados, between Bridgetown and the airport, with a string of small villages offering a variety of accommodation and places to eat. There are excellent white sand beaches all along this stretch of coast, and the sea is calm pretty much all year round. **St Lawrence Gap** is the main tourist drag, with an active nightlife and a plethora of hotels, guesthouses and restaurants; **Hastings**, **Rockley** and **Worthing** are a little less lively but all have their charm, while the quieter **Silver Sands** further east mostly pulls in a crowd of young windsurfers. The fishing town of **Oistins** – the biggest town in the parish – is the one spot in the area that retains a local feel, although it's increasingly attracting tourists for the superb fish dinners served from a dozen tiny shacks in the atmospheric town centre.

One negative effect of all the development in the area has been the severe damage inflicted on the **environment**. You'll probably notice the shortage of vegetation, chopped down first for the sugar plantations, more recently for the construction of tourist facilities and residential development. The coral reefs that used to proliferate offshore have also been a casualty, with pollution and overfishing taking a dramatic toll; as a result, the south coast beaches, once protected by the reefs, have suffered heavy erosion over the last couple of decades. However, belated steps are being taken to improve matters: artificial reefs have been laid to protect the coastline and, near Worthing, the tiny **Graeme Hall Swamp** – habitat of a multitude of birds and an important marine breeding ground – has been designated a protected area.

HASTINGS AND ROCKLEY

Map 4 B5.

A short ride east of Bridgetown, **HASTINGS** first developed in the eighteenth century as a by-product of Britain's military development of the nearby Garrison Savannah (see

Chattel Houses

Vacant land was in short supply in nineteenth-century Barbados. Most of the tiny island was given over to sugar production, and the landless poor who worked on the plantations invariably had to live on the owner's land. Forever at risk of being evicted – in which case they would lose their homes – the workers devised a mobile house which could be taken to pieces and rebuilt elsewhere should the need arise. From the legal term "chattel", meaning a moveable possession, these houses became known as **chattel houses**.

The first chattel houses were built from planks of cheap pine, imported from North America in pre-cut lengths, and rested on limestone blocks to provide an even foundation. The facades were symmetrical, with a central door flanked by two windows; the roof was steeply gabled and the windows were jalousied to allow air to circulate and to give the house stability during hurricanes. The interiors were small, usually divided into two rooms, but as the owners garnered a bit more money, they would take the back off the house to add an extra, identical unit or a shed with a flat roof. Another popular addition was a small veranda at the front, while those with an artistic inclination (and the cash) would add fretwork over the doors and windows and maybe a hood above the window to keep rain out.

Today, with no need to move a house from place to place any longer, few chattel houses are built, although their attractive design remains popular and their influence can be seen in larger houses in affluent areas of Bridgetown and in tourist bars and restaurants across the island.

p.52). Soldiers from St Ann's Fort were quartered here – you can still see the red-brick buildings on your left as you enter the town – and a naval hospital and the Admiral's quarters were built south of here beside the coast. More than a century later, its proximity to the capital led to Hastings being developed as Barbados's first tourist resort, and a handful of grand old hotels still stand on the seafront to mark those glory days. Sadly, the once attractive beach has been heavily eroded, and the whole place now wears a somewhat forlorn expression; you'll probably want to pass straight through, although there are a couple of nightspots (see p.149).

A couple of miles further along Highway 7, **ROCKLEY**'s main attraction is its magnificent beach, known locally as **Accra Beach** – a great white swathe of sand, popular with tourists and local families, that can get pretty crowded at peak season and weekends. Hair-braiders, T-shirt and craft vendors and the odd hustler mingle with the windsurfers and sun-ripening tourists to create one of the liveliest beach scenes on the island – it's a good place just to sit back and people-watch. Behind the beach, there are a couple of decent places to stay, though much of the main highway that runs through Rockley has been given over to garish fast-food joints and reeks of over-development. Higher up, away from the beach and rarely seen by tourists, some of the island's most exclusive residential districts offer prime commuting territory for bankers, lawyers and other professionals working in Bridgetown.

WORTHING

Map 4, E5.

Like the Victorian seaside resort in England after which it is named, the once elegant village of **WORTHING** is now tatty and faded, but its easygoing feel and handful of decent, inexpensive guesthouses make it a popular target for budget travellers. There's a gleaming white beach, less crowded than Accra Beach further west but just as enjoyable, with a couple of laid-back bars, a string of vendors hanging up their T-shirts and batik prints, and a few local guys offering boat-trips and waverunner rentals. St Lawrence Gap, just five minutes' walk away (see below), offers more in the way of restaurants and nightlife, but Worthing is a very likeable alternative if you want to escape the crowd. Highway 7 runs through the village, with a string of shops, banks and supermarkets on its north side and all of the accommodation to the south.

GRAEME HALL SWAMP

Map 4, E4.

Less than a kilometre to the northeast of Worthing, the **Graeme Hall Swamp** is one of the few remaining areas of mangrove swamp on the island – an important eco-system, providing shelter for a variety of migratory birds and a nursery for many types of fish, protected from predators in the shallow waters. The water runs under the main road east of town and down to the sea, where its flow is controlled by a sluice-gate. Beside the road, a damp path leads into the swamp for 500m out the mangroves, with their huge aerial roots, and do a bit of bird spotting.

Northwest of Worthing, stargazers can make for the **Harry Bayley Observatory** (open 4 or 5 nights each month; ©426 1317 for times; free). Built in 1963, the place is headquarters of the Barbados Astronomical Society and the only observatory in the West Indies.

ST LAWRENCE GAP

Map 4, E5.

Just past Worthing, a right-hand turn takes you off the main road to run along the coast for a kilometre or so, passing through the heavily touristed **ST LAWRENCE GAP** and **Dover** before rejoining the main road near Maxwell. The most developed area of the south coast – with hotels, restaurants, tourist shops and vendors strung out along virtually the entire road – this is something of a tourist enclave; you'll see few Bajans here, other than those who work in the industry. Still, it's a laid-back place with more great beaches, particularly in front of the giant *Divi Southwinds* time-share resort, although erosion has taken its toll in a few spots east and west of the hotel. None of the buses or minibuses run through the Gap, so you'll need to get your walking boots on if you're heading in.

St Lawrence Gap is the main strip for restaurants and nightlife, and always has a busy scene in the evening. Recently, a few local hustlers have moved in – mostly selling drugs – though they're rarely over-pushy, and undercover cops are often on hand to nab the most persistent. If you're here in April during the Congaline festival (see p.171), the football field at Dover normally gets taken over by food and drink stalls and crowds of people, and there's a great party atmosphere.

MAXWELL

Map 4, I4.

There's not much to **MAXWELL**, a kilometre or so east of St Lawrence, and it's easy to drive straight through on Highway 7 without noticing it. It's not a bad choice as a place to stay, though there's no reason to stop otherwise. A couple of the hotels (see p.134) are on the highway, but most are just south of it on the Maxwell Coast Road which makes a small loop off the main road. The beaches here are as good as those further west, but there's little sense of community and it can feel rather cut off in the evenings. The area is popular with windsurfers, particularly beginners/intermediates (experts head east to Silver Sands), and boards can be rented from *Club Mistral*, beside the *Windsurf Village Hotel*, for US$20 an hour, $55 for a half-day. Coaching is also given, though prices are exorbitant.

For further details of watersports in the area and throughout Barbados, see p.173.

OISTINS

Map 4, K4.

Continuing east from Maxwell brings you into **OISTINS**, the main town along the south coast and one of its less touristed parts. A couple of **buses** run here from Bridgetown, as does **route taxi** 11, which continues to Silver Sands. The unusual name is a corruption of Austin, who was one of the first landowners in the area. It's a busy little town, dominated by a central fish market and retaining an authentic sense of Barbados before the tourist boom. The best time to visit is in the evening, when a dozen small shacks in the central Bay Garden sell fried fish straight out of the boats, and on Friday nights hundreds of people descend for a "lime", the local term for a social gathering.

OISTINS

The annual Oistins Fish Festival, held every March, celebrates the town's fishing tradition, with boat races and fish-boning tournaments.

Christ Church Parish Church is high up north of town; to get there, follow the main road as it swings northeast out of town and turn left up Church Hill. The present squat, turreted coral block building is the church's fifth incarnation, the others having been destroyed by fire and hurricane over the centuries. Inside, there's a modern stained-glass window behind the altar, a series of plaster reliefs along the walls and an attractive mahogany gallery at the back. The sprawling cemetery that surrounds the church is a little more interesting, with plenty of intriguing, crumbling tombs amid the frangipani and sago palms. The **Chase family vault**, on the south side, has the most peculiar history. Three times during the 1810s the vault was opened for a new burial, only to find that the lead coffins had mysteriously shifted from their original position. When this happened a fourth time, after the vault had been officially locked under the Governor's seal, the coffins were taken out and buried elsewhere in the churchyard.

Miami Beach

Map 2, D9.

There's no beach of note in Oistins itself, but several are just a couple of minutes away. As you head east, take the right hand turn-off for Enterprise and another right is soon signposted for the Enterprise Coast Road, offering a fabulous drive beside the sea. Turn right again for **Miami Beach** – a lovely stretch dotted with casuarina trees that marks the last protected beach before you round the headland for the exposed central and eastern beaches – or left past the South Point lighthouse for Silver Sands and Long Beach.

Silver Sands and Long Beach

Map 2, E9.
Silver Sands is famous for windsurfing, and attracts surfers from all over the world, though non-surfers come here too for the quiet, easygoing vibe. Fantastic waves roll in for most of the year and there are a handful of (pretty expensive) places where you can rent a windsurfer if you haven't brought your own. The beaches are less busy than further west – mainly because of the often choppy seas – but equally attractive; true to its name, **Long Beach**, just beyond the *Ocean Spray Apartments*, is the longest beach on the island – a huge stretch of crunchy white sand strewn with driftwood – and is often completely deserted.

....
For more on watersports, see p.173.
....

For more on watersports, see p.173.

St Philip

The largest parish on the island, but with less than half the population of Christ Church, **St Philip** has a different feel from its more touristed neighbour, with no crowds, far less development and a general sense of isolation. The coastline here is much more rugged than you'll find further west, with only a handful of white sand beaches – several of them, especially **Crane Bay** and **Bottom Bay**, quite

ST PHILIP

spectacular – divided from each other by long cliffs and rocky outcrops. The sea is much rougher too, with Atlantic waves crashing in all year round; bear this in mind if you are thinking of staying out here since, though there are several places where you can swim safely, you may get tired of the pounding surf. Even if you're not staying, there are a handful of attractions worth making for, including a couple of old houses, a spanking new rum factory and a small zoo.

If you're relying on public transport, buses run along the south coast road as far as *Sam Lord's Castle*, passing the *Crane Beach Hotel*, though if you're heading for any of the beaches, you'll need to walk down to them from the main road – usually around 500m.

FOUL BAY AND CRANE BEACH

Map 2, G8.
Three or four kilometres beyond the airport, **FOUL BAY** is the largest beach on this section of the coast. Access isn't signposted; look out for the large Methodist Church beside the road in the small village of Rice and turn 100m further on takes you right down to the beach. It's a long, wide white sand beach with a handful of fishing boats normally pulled up on its eastern side, and you'll find few tourists (and no food and drink facilities). The long cliffs give the place a rugged feel but it's not particularly pretty – if you're after a more picturesque 'dream' beach, you may want to head for Bottom Bay, a little further east (see p.70).

Back on the main road, the **Crane Beach Hotel** lies half a kilometre beyond Foul Bay. This was one of the first hotels on the island and still commands a superb site above Crane Bay. During the eighteenth century, when the offshore reef offered rather more protection than it does now, there was a small commercial port here, and a large crane perched on the cliff edge raised and lowered cargo to the ships below. A house was erected in 1790 and today forms the east wing; during the 1880s the place was converted into a hotel, whose early guests included 'Wild Bill' Hickock.

It's a very fetching place and worth a look even if you're not staying (a B$5 is charged for use of the facilities, though you can put the entry fee towards any food or drinks you have during your visit – and if you're here before 10am you'll probably arrive in time to avoid paying). A long Roman-style swimming pool runs alongside the main hotel building at the top of the cliff and, beside the panoramic restaurant, two hundred steps lead down to a pretty beach. Various writers have waxed lyrical over this beach during the last century, but hurricane damage has altered its shape and it is no longer quite as fabulous as they once claimed. On the other side of the pool, a walkway cut into the rock also winds down to the ocean – this was first cut during the 1760s to provide a discreet bathing spot for women.

....

For details on staying at the
Crane Beach Hotel, **see p.136.**

....

SAM LORD'S CASTLE

Map 2, G7. Open to non-residents daily 9am–5pm.

Five minutes' drive east of Crane Bay, **SAM LORD'S CASTLE** is a much larger hotel, spread out above a couple of decent beaches in the island's southeastern corner. The place is open to anyone, though non-residents are supposed to pay an entrance fee of B$12 (redeemable at any of the hotel's bars or restaurants) for access to it and the beach. The hotel buildings spread out around a central mansion – the 'castle' – built in 1820 by Sam Lord, a legendary local crook who reputedly made his fortune from luring ships onto the nearby reef and salvaging anything of value. Though the story is questioned by local historians, there is no doubt that Lord made a lot of money from one dubious source or another and spent much of it building his home here. Parts of the house were built by craftsmen from England in the style of Windsor Castle and the downstairs rooms – all on show – are expensively furnished and decorated.

For details on staying at *Sam Lord's Castle*, see p.136.

HARRISMITH AND BOTTOM BAY

Map 2, G7.
Beyond Sam Lord's Castle there are a couple of good beaches worth checking out. Head out of the castle and take the first right up to the main road, then turn right again. After 500m or so there is a right turn marked "Harrismith". Follow the road down and turn left along a rutted track just before you reach a couple of casuarina trees. At the bottom of the track is the **Harrismith Great House**; after serving time as a hotel, it is now deserted. The building commands a grand site over Harrismith beach, with steps leading down just west of the house. However, **BOTTOM BAY**, 500m further east, is still more spectacular; go back to the main road, turn right and the turning is signposted on the right. Park at the top of the cliffs and walk down the steps to the small

sugar-white beach, sandwiched between the cliffs, with a backdrop of palm trees and the Atlantic waves crashing in. Few people find the place, although locals use it at the weekend and the occasional tour bus heads this way on Wednesdays.

THE FOURSQUARE RUM FACTORY AND HERITAGE PARK

Map 2, F8. Mon–Thurs 10am–6pm, Fri–Sat 10am–9pm, Sun noon–6pm; B$20.

Smack in the middle of the sweeping fields of sugarcane that dominate the interior of St Philip, the **Foursquare Rum Factory and Heritage Park** is an ultra-modern rum distillery built in the 1990s on the site of an ancient sugar estate. The factory combines state-of-the-art design with traditional features and buildings, and the compulsory forty-minute tour is an interesting introduction to the production of sugar and its chief by-product – rum – particularly if you haven't already been round any of the rum factories near Bridgetown (see p.48). There's also a small, attractive art museum on site and a number of shops and snack-bars.

Tours start with a short video about Bajan rum-making and the history of the Foursquare sugar plantation, established in the 1640s, during the earliest days of sugar on Barbados. Windmills were built to crush the sugarcane grown on the estate, and a factory soon followed, where the juice of the sugarcane was boiled to produce thick, dark molasses that were exported to feed the increasingly sweet English tooth. By the 1860s it was steam-driven, and produced sugar rather than molasses for export. As throughout

Barbados, the factory was modified over the ensuing century as the world demand for sugar was declining but, by 1988, it had lost the battle and was closed.

After the video, the tour moves on through the gleaming factory, where the guides point out the modern boilers and fermentation tanks and explain how the rum is produced. You'll also see the older parts of the factory that have been incorporated into the design of the modern rum distillery, including an old fire-brick boiler, installed in 1910 and built from bricks used as ballast by British schooners that traded with the island at the turn of the century.

For more about the traditional rum industry of Barbados, see p.49.

At the end of the tour, your guide will hand you a miniature bottle of white rum and leave you beside the 250-year-old art foundry, a long, elegant building of thick coral stone blocks that once housed part of the sugar factory. Today, the place serves as a trendy art gallery, featuring paintings and sculptures by Bajan artists and occasional exhibitions of work from around the Caribbean. Most of the pieces are for sale, and you can also buy bottles of the *ESA Field* rum made in the factory. Outside the foundry, pieces of the factory's old machinery are scattered around the site; elsewhere, there's a variety of craft studios making and selling wicker baskets, leather bags, and jewellery, and stalls selling snacks and drinks.

SUNBURY PLANTATION HOUSE

Map 2, E7. Daily 10am–5pm; B$12.
Northwest of Sam Lord's Castle and signposted off the main road just above the small town of Six Cross Roads,

Sunbury Plantation House is one of the oldest and – for the sheer variety of furniture, island prints and colonial-era bits and pieces – one of the most interesting of the island's great houses. Your entry fee gets you a guided tour of the interior, after which you're free to wander at your leisure through the main rooms and around the extensive gardens; there's a small outdoor café at the back of the house if you fancy a snack once you've finished exploring.

Ownership of the sugar estate here goes back to a Matthew Chapman, one of the very first settlers in Barbados, although the plantation house itself (and the name Sunbury, after the owners' home in England) date from the mid-eighteenth century. Badly damaged during the 1816 slave revolt (see p.75), Sunbury was purchased for £33,000 in 1835 by a local shipping merchant, Thomas Daniel, whose descendants retained ownership of the place until 1981. Daniel was a friend of the notorious Sam Lord (see p.70) – a regular visitor here – and acted as Lord's go-between with his estranged wife after she fled to England to escape his brutal treatment.

The building has recently been restored after being gutted by fire in 1995, and looks almost exactly as it did (a photograph album shows the house before, during and after). Although only the walls are original, built with local coral blocks and ballast from British ships and made 50cm thick to withstand hurricane winds, the restorers have done a brilliant job in recapturing the period feel of the rooms, helped by donations of furniture and other artefacts from across the island. There is a wealth of old mahogany pieces on the ground floor, with the massive claw-footed dining table taking pride of place, while the walls are lined with prints and paintings of old Barbados. Upstairs, the bedrooms show off nineteenth-century fashions; down-

SUNBURY PLANTATION HOUSE

stairs, the cellars are stuffed with paraphernalia from traditional plantation life, including horse-drawn buggies, cooking pots, cutlery and the sad, charred relics of the 1995 fire.

OUGHTERSON GREAT HOUSE AND ZOO

Map 2, F7. Daily 9.30am–4.30pm; B$12

Head east from Sunbury and the country roads wind through the sugar fields to the small zoo park at **Oughterson Great House**. En route, you'll pass **Daphne's Sea Shell Studio** (Mon–Fri 9am–5pm, Sat 9am–4pm), a small gift shop based in the rebuilt cowshed of another old plantation house and worth checking out for its inventive (though not cheap) arrangements of shells and hand-painted shirts.

The Georgian great house was badly damaged in the the 1816 slave revolt (see box), when workers from the local sugar plantations rose up against their masters, and by the hurricane of 1831, and most of it dates from subsequent rebuilding. The squat, ochre house is actually no longer part of the adjacent plantation, which was hived off when purchased by the current owners, but if you're interested in the history, the managers can show you copies of contemporaneous letters written by local white militiamen which capture some of the mood of the time, criticizing anti-slavery campaigner William Wilberforce and the dangerous hopes he was raising among slaves (see p.193). You can wander through the ground floor, though most of it is roped off and the only things you can inspect close up are a few antique chests, rocking chairs and eighteenth-century prints of the island.

You're really here for the slightly bizarre zoo at the back of the house – the only one on the island – which features

Bussa's Rebellion

In 1807 the British government banned the transfer of slaves from Africa to the Caribbean. The measure had little immediate impact on the Barbadian planters, who preferred creole slaves born on the island, but it fuelled the growing movement for the abolition of slavery itself. In an attempt to deflect criticism, Barbadian planters made some token improvements to the slaves' conditions: women's working hours were reduced; whites could be punished for the murder of a black; and slaves were permitted to own property.

But the slaves correctly perceived that none of this was conceded willingly. Rumours spread, claiming that emancipation had been proclaimed in Britain but was being blocked on the island. Frustration grew, and in April 1816 Barbados faced its only serious slave uprising. Bussa's Rebellion – named after its leader, an African-born slave who was head ranger at a plantation in St Philip – began in the southeast with attacks on property and widespread burning of the sugar fields. It quickly spread throughout the southern and central parishes, and the slaves fought several battles against the white militias and British troops. They never stood a chance: within three days the rebellion was crushed, with only a handful of white casualties but over a thousand slaves either killed in battle or executed afterwards, along with prominent free coloured supporters of emancipation. There were no further outbreaks of violence, but the abolitionist movement in Britain grew until slavery was finally ended in 1834.

Brazilian tapirs, zebras, alligators, snakes, monkeys and parrots (including some very rare species from neighbouring islands which are bred in captivity here). There is also a small aquarium in the old kitchen, probably the oldest part of the great house. Your appreciation of the place will obviously depend on how comfortable you feel seeing animals in captivity; bear in mind too that, during the heat of the day, almost everything will be asleep.

THE WEST COAST

Barbados's "platinum coast" is a fringe of bays and coves along the sheltered, Caribbean side of the island. Its sandy beaches and warm blue waters have made it the island's prime resort area. As a result, the coastline has been heavily built-up; it holds the island's top golf courses and priciest hotels, and its sought-after private homes change hands at formidable prices.

However, you don't need to win the lottery to visit. There's a smattering of reasonably priced places to stay and, as everywhere on Barbados, all of the beaches are public. Admittedly, it's a bit of a tramp to reach a few of them, but there are many which are well worth a visit, particularly those at **Prospect**, **Sandy Lane** and **Mullins Bay**. If you're into some serious exercise it's even possible to walk most of the way along the coast at low tide.

If you can drag yourself away from the beach, the region has other attractions. Lively, modern **Holetown** has a fine old church and a legion of shopping opportunities, while further north, **Speightstown** repays a visit for the colonial relics and picturesque old streets that recall its vanished heyday as a major port. A short detour inland, through fields of sugarcane and tiny farming villages, will take you to the small art gallery at **Bagatelle Great House** and the sugar museum at **Portvale**.

Getting there and getting around

It could hardly be easier to get around on the west coast. North of Bridgetown, Highway 1 runs up the coast, rarely straying more than 100m from the shoreline. Highway 2A runs parallel to it, some way inland, and offers a speedier way of getting to the north of the island.

Buses and minibuses ply the coast road between Bridgetown and Speightstown all day, and there are bus stops every couple of hundred metres. Services normally stop at around midnight, after which you'll need a car or private taxi. If you're coming from the south coast, look for buses marked "Speightstown" – these usually bypass Bridgetown and save you having to change buses (and terminals) in the city.

For details of west coast accommodation, see p.137.

NORTH TO PROSPECT

There is little sign of the hotel extravaganza to come as Highway 1 begins to carve its way up the west coast through the tiny village of **PROSPECT**. Most of the accommodation here is residential and the beaches – largely bereft of tourists – are popular at weekends and holidays with families up from Bridgetown. **Betts Rock Park** – a left turn just before the Portobello Gallery (see below) – is a large, slightly scruffy beach zone with a couple of lifeguard towers and a picnic area. A better bet, if you want to swim, is **Prospect Beach**, a little further up the coast – a narrow crescent of sand, backed by manchineel trees and palms, and a calm turquoise bay. Public access is via a path just north of the all-inclusive *Escape*

Hotel, and at busy times the beach can get crowded with the hotel's guests.

Portobello Gallery

Map 5, C10. Daily 9am–4pm; B$5.

Cautiously hidden behind iron bars and guard dogs, the small **Portobello Gallery** – in a beautiful location overlooking the ocean – specializes in art from Haiti and has around a hundred paintings on display. You probably won't want to buy – prices are exorbitant, bordering on the absurd – but there's an interesting selection and it's a good introduction to the country's distinctive art. You'll see cheaper, derivative stuff at souvenir shops around the island.

BAGATELLE GREAT HOUSE

Map 5, D8. Daily 9am–5pm; free.

Continuing north, there is little to distinguish this area of coast other than a series of superlative bays and beaches, many of them tucked away behind an increasingly grand row of hotels and private mansions, themselves often hidden by security fences.

A right turn opposite the *Tamarind Cove Hotel* winds up into the island's interior, past the grand polo field at **Holder's House** – an old great house and the venue for a prestigious music festival every March (see below). Once you reach the main road, turn left for the **Bagatelle Great House** – one of the best examples of early Barbadian vernacular architecture. A classic double staircase leads up to the old living quarters, fronted by a columned porch with a decorated pediment, while the entrance below the porch leads into deep cellars which once served as the house's food stores.

Holder's Festival

Founded in 1993, the Caribbean's leading **festival of classical music** is now held annually in March at Holder's House, a gorgeous old plantation house just inland from Sandy Lane Bay. If you're familiar with the reggae festivals of Jamaica, or Carnival in Trinidad, you may find it somewhat incongruous to find operas and classical concerts being performed in period costume outdoors under the mahogany and palm trees. But little expense is spared – quality singers and musicians are flown in specially from Britain – and the spectacular setting invests the whole thing with a magical air.

The owners generally put together an imaginative schedule: 1997, for example, saw the restaging after 170 years of *Inkle and Yarico* – an eighteenth-century opera about a traditional Barbadian legend that was once all the rage in London's West End – as well as a concert by Pavarotti and, away from the classical sphere, a festival of calypso music with contributions by top performers from Trinidad and Barbados. If you're interested, contact the Barbados Tourism Authority or Holders House direct on © (246) 432 6385, fax (246) 432 6461.

According to tradition, the name of the great house derives from a former owner who, having lost the estate in a dice game, derided it as "a mere bagatelle". Today the old cellars serve as the venue for a fashionable restaurant, while the rooms upstairs hold occasional displays of local art.

SANDY LANE

Map 5, B7.

Back on the coast, the road through the area of Sandy Lane Bay is overhung with lush vegetation and reeks of wealth. In

Barbados, the name **Sandy Lane** is synonymous with the grandest of the island's hotels – a byword for Caribbean affluence and ostentation, with a list of repeat celebrity guests as long as your arm. Built in the early 1960s by Anglo-American Ronald Tree, a former parliamentary adviser to the government of Sir Winston Churchill, the hotel was designed to provide a winter retreat for the British upper classes, and the surrounding land was bought up for private homes for Tree's friends. Today, the likes of Joan Collins, Mick Jagger and Michael Caine are regular winter visitors, but the place guards its guests jealously behind high walls and security guards.

Nevertheless, as part of his deal with the government to get permission for the hotel (and the rerouting of the coastal road that it involved), Tree promised to provide a ten-metre right of way to the south of the property, giving public access to the shore. Today that access is still there and, if you've got the energy, you can wander down to the bay past the tall casuarinas and manchineel trees. The sweep of gently shelving sand, backed by the elegant and surprisingly unflashy coralstone hotel, is quite magnificent.

HOLETOWN

Map 5, C6.

It was in present-day **HOLETOWN** that English sailors first landed in Barbados in 1625, claiming the island for their king, James I, and naming the area St James' Town before moving on. Two years later the *William and John* landed at the same spot carrying a party of settlers; they renamed the place Holetown because an inlet from the sea – where they could anchor their shallow-draft ships – reminded them of the Hole on the River Thames in

London. The place developed slowly, quickly losing favour to the site of present-day Bridgetown, whose natural harbours offered better protection for shipping.

The town

Today, Holetown is the third-largest town in Barbados – a busy, modern hub for the local tourist industry, if somewhat lacking in character. All west coast buses run through the town, and the main highway is lined with fast-food restaurants, souvenir shops, banks and grocery stores. Just before you reach the centre, **Sunset Crest** is a large shopping area on the east side of the highway with plenty of souvenir shops selling T-shirts, books and liquor. There are a couple of places where you can cut down to the beach, though the sand is often crowded and narrow here and you're better off heading out of town if you want to swim.

On the west side of the highway, the police station is built on the site of the old **James Fort**, a few of whose iron cannons still sit outside, next to an obelisk erected in 1905 to commemorate the 300th anniversary of the arrival of the first settlers. Unfortunately, the historians of the time were 22 years out with their calculations, though this didn't stop them from enjoying a huge celebratory street party. An unapologetic corrective plaque was quietly fixed to the obelisk in 1977 to mark the 350th anniversary.

A few minutes' walk north of here, 1st and 2nd Streets, lined with trendy restaurants, lead down to the sea. Continuing north, also alongside the highway, the **chattel house village** has a dozen reproduction chattel houses selling gifts and souvenirs. Further on, the scenery becomes more bucolic, with fields, cows and a cricket pitch by the roadside; a road bridge runs over the **Hole**, which is alive with egrets towards sunset.

For details of the best places to eat and drink in Holetown, see p.159.

St James's Parish Church

Map 5, C6.

Five minutes' walk further on is **St James's Parish Church,** one of the most attractive on the island. It is also the oldest religious site in Barbados – the original wooden church was built here in 1628. It was replaced by a stone structure in 1660 but, as happened throughout the island, hurricane and fire damage took their toll. As a consequence, most of the present building, including the elegant round tower above the altar, dates from between 1789 and 1874, when the nave was extended by six metres. However, there are older relics: the stone pillars at the entrance to the south porch are thought to date from the seventeenth century, while the baptismal font and the iron bell in the north porch bear the dates 1684 and 1696 respectively.

The present church is a small but graceful building, with thick stone walls, and two columns supporting the stone chancel arch that divides the nave from the choir. There are the usual marble funerary monuments on the walls, while more modern works of art include a colourful biblical triptych by Ethiopian painter Alemayehu Bizumeh and bronze bas-reliefs of St James and St Mary by Czech sculptor George Kveton. There are also extracts from the church's old register of births and deaths, which show the short life expectancy of the early settlers, and a letter from the White House expressing Ronald and Nancy Reagan's appreciation of a service they attended here in 1982. Reagan's currying of favour with Caribbean leaders paid dividends a year later when the majority – headed by Barbados's Tom Adams – gave avid support to the US invasion of Grenada.

FOLKESTONE MARINE PARK

Map 5, B6. Mon–Sat 9am–4pm; B\$1.

Five minutes' walk north of St James's Parish Church, the visitor centre at **Folkestone Marine Park** has a short video film and a handful of reasonable displays on the island's coral reefs and other marine life. The park, established in 1979, extends down the coast as far as Sandy Lane Bay. It used to contain an underwater trail for snorkellers, though sadly this has been damaged by storms. There is talk of recreating it, however, and if you want to head for the offshore reef you can usually find a glass-bottomed boat and snorkelling gear. If you're just into loafing around, the beach outside the visitor centre – a decent if narrow and rather rocky patch, backed by casuarina and manchineel trees – is popular with local families on weekends and holidays, and has a lifeguard, showers, snack-bars and a sprinkling of beach vendors.

PORTVALE SUGAR MUSEUM

Map 5, E6. Mon–Sat 9am–5pm; B\$8.

A couple of miles inland from Holetown, the informative **Portvale Sugar Museum** – signposted off Highway 2A just north of the main roundabout – offers a clear introduction to the product on which Barbados depended for nearly three hundred years, before charter planes started to deliver the tourists who now account for more than half of the island's GNP. The small museum is the brainchild of Frank Hutson, a former sugar worker, who rescued a load of rusting sugar-mill machinery from dump sites across the island,

A typical bar in downtown Bridgetown

A palm-shaded beach on the island's southeast coast

Driftwood frames a lifeguard's tower on Crane Beach

The rugged and wind-lashed east coast near Bathsheba

The seventeenth-century plantation house, St Nicholas Abbey

Atlantic breakers pound the island's rocky northern tip

IAN CUMMING

A meeting of the Progressive Ballroom Dancing Society in Bridgetown

IAN CUMMING

Sunset at Mullins Bay, on the island's calm Caribbean west coast

The story of sugar

Commercial **sugar production** started in Barbados in 1643, using plants introduced from Brazil by Dutch traders, and heralded a dramatic change in the island's fortunes. The original dense forest that covered the island was chopped down to leave bare land suitable for the new plantations, and the frontier farming communities of European migrants were replaced by a slave-based plantation society as Africans were brought in to labour in the sugar fields.

Barbados was England's first sugar-producing colony, and it provided fabulous returns for plantation owners for well over a century. Though the island gradually lost ground to the nearby production centre of Jamaica, tax and trade incentives meant that growing sugar remained lucrative, and the planters celebrated their wealth by building the lavish great houses that still overlook the cane fields from breezy hilltop perches. However, the industry took two big hits in the mid-nineteenth century when the abolition of the slave trade in 1834 was followed by the British Sugar Equalization Act of 1846, which ended preferential treatment for sugar produced in the colonies.

Though no longer able to compete effectively with cheaper sugar from Cuba and Brazil, the Barbadian sugar industry rumbled on into the twentieth century. Over recent decades, attempts to save the industry have included centralization of factories and the introduction of modern mechanization. Though the windmills are no longer turning, the swaying fields of cane that still dominate the island remain testament to the continuing importance of King Sugar.

PORTVALE SUGAR MUSEUM

cleaned it up and incorporated it into the museum with captions, maps and photos explaining the role of sugar on the island since its introduction in the 1640s.

The museum is housed in the former boiling house of the local Blowers sugar estate, built in the 1880s, and its main exhibit is the series of "tayches" or boiling pans in which the cane juice was heated, with the scum or waste floating to the top and being ladled off, before the residue was passed into the next, smaller pan en route to being turned into crystals. Elsewhere, there are giant pieces of mill machinery, as well as the tools of the blacksmiths and coopers who helped to keep the sugar estates running smoothly, but it is the old black and white photos that best evoke the era in which sugar was king – workers slaving in the fields, grinding the cane and racing the barrels of sugar through the streets of Bridgetown to catch the next boat to England.

Between February and May, the entrance price rises to B$15 to include a tour of the adjacent sugar factory – a heady experience for the smell alone – where you can view the full production process, from the loading and grinding of the cane to the crystallization of the brown sugar, which is sent off for refining abroad. The factory was built in 1984 and, during its relatively short operating season, takes cane from 33 local plantations and more than six hundred small farmers.

NORTH TO MULLINS BAY

Map 5, B3.

Once you've passed Folkestone, there is little of particular interest to hold you en route north to Speightstown. **Glitter Bay** is the last of the series of exclusive hotels and is followed by a series of grand private houses, fenced in behind security gates, interspersed with small villages of shops, fishing shacks and chattel houses, keeping a typically Bajan toehold on the increasingly developed west coast.

Access to many of the small bays along the coast is difficult, but **Mullins Bay** – a strip of sugary sand with a lively beach bar – is a good place to stop for a swim. Buses stop here and there's a car park across from the bay. If it's crowded, wander off down the beach to find your own private spot.

SPEIGHTSTOWN

Map 5, B2.

Small, run-down and utterly charming, **SPEIGHT-STOWN** (pronounced 'Spikestown') is the second town of Barbados, though it remains largely untouched by tourist development. It was once a thriving port, famous for its tough-talking, uncompromising inhabitants – 'Speightstown flattery' is an old Bajan term for a back-handed compliment. Over the last century, however, the place has declined precipitately, and there is little to do today but stroll around and soak up the remnants of the local fishing industry, a few stylish old buildings and a handful of excellent restaurants that cater for day visitors and the residents of the nearby all-inclusive hotels.

Buses running up the west coast normally terminate at Speightstown, stopping at the eastern end of Church Street – from here, head down towards the sea and you'll pass the parish church on your right. Queen Street has an unofficial tourist information office in the *Fisherman's Pub* (see p.161).

Some history

Speightstown was founded around 1635, named after William Speight, a rich merchant, landowner and general bigwig, and soon became one of the island's most important **ports**, exporting indigo, cotton, ginger and tobacco from fields in the north. As Barbados grew more prosperous, Speightstown – dubbed Little Bristol for its connections with the great port city in England – began to trade vast quantities of **sugar and molasses** with the home country. Ships sailing from Bristol brought bricks as ballast in their empty holds (soon to be filled with Bajan produce), providing the material for a number of grand buildings around town. In the days before proper roads and cars, Speightstown also did a roaring trade with Bridgetown; schooners carried passengers and cargo between the two in just 45 minutes. The port brought in great wealth, and merchants built warehouses along the waterfront to hold the shipments, and stores along the main streets selling provisions for the ships and fine wines for the rich traders.

However, with the development of major port facilities at Bridgetown – and of good roads, which made it cheaper to transport produce and people to the capital by car and lorry – Speightstown's domestic and international trade dried up. The town went into **decline**, the old buildings were left to decay, and a great fire in 1941 destroyed many historic quarters. Recent years have seen ambitious proposals to preserve and recreate Speightstown's historic character, turning it into a "model town". For the time being, however, it remains an earthy, beguiling place, with old-fashioned Georgian-style shops fronting onto narrow streets, their galleries – propped up on wooden pillars – projecting out over the pavements.

The town

A mark of Speightstown's former importance is that three major forts were erected to protect it, with several additional

Ayscue's invasion

Many of the early settlers in Barbados came from England to escape the civil war between king and parliament that traumatized the country in the 1640s. The majority of those who fled were Royalists, and after the defeat and execution of King Charles I in 1649, they proclaimed his son Charles II as their ruler. In retaliation for this insubordination, England's parliament promptly sent a fleet under the command of Sir George Ayscue to subdue the island.

In December 1651, Ayscue launched an invasion at Speightstown. Despite losing men to musket fire on the town's pristine beaches, the invaders were better equipped and soon overcame the local defenders. Peace terms were signed at the Mermaid Tavern in Oistins on January 11, 1652, and became known as the "Charter of Barbados". This document obliged Bajans to accept the authority of the English parliament but also, crucially, stated that no taxes could be raised on local people without their consent. This retention of the power of purse meant that, from the island's early days, the affairs of Barbados were largely controlled by Bajans rather than the English.

gun emplacements scattered along the coast to add to the barrage of any enemy ships (though the only invasion was by English forces in 1651, see box above). Little remains of the military hardware, though some of the old iron cannons from Fort Orange point out to sea from **the Esplanade**, to the north of town.

St Peter's Parish Church

Across from the Esplanade, **St Peter's Parish Church**, on Church Street, was first built in the 1630s, making it one of

ST PETER'S PARISH CHURCH

the oldest churches in Barbados. Destroyed by the 1831 hurricane, the Georgian building was rebuilt in a graceful Greek revival style – though with the standard tower tacked on for good measure – and the present incarnation was superbly restored after the place was gutted by fire in 1980.

Queen Street

Back on the main road, head south across the bridge and past the fish market, always humming with vendors in the early morning. **Queen Street** is the main drag and has several grand old buildings that have just about survived the town's decline. Opposite *Mango's* restaurant, the grey, peeling and rather decayed-looking **Arlington**, almost medieval in design, is a classic example of the island's early town-houses – narrow, tall and gabled, with a sharply sloping roof. The iron gateway and outside staircase were common among the houses of the wealthy Speightstown merchants; this one probably belonged to a ship's chandler, with a shop downstairs and the family home on the two floors above.

Arlington is likely to be one of the first beneficiaries of the proposed revamping of Speightstown but, for now, it's still worth a quick look for a stark image of old Barbados. While you're here, check out the nearby art gallery of the self-styled Gang of Four – worth a look for the local paintings of Gordon Webster and Sarah Venables and the sculpture of Ras Bongo Congo. If you're here at night, the art gallery above the *Mango* restaurant is also worth a quick visit.

For details of the best places to eat and drink in Speightstown, see p.161.

CENTRAL
BARBADOS

D on't expect dramatic topographical change as you head into the **interior of Barbados**; the landscape of the central parishes of **St George** and **St Thomas** is almost uniformly flat or gently rolling – perfect for the sugar crop that's been under cultivation here for almost four centuries. As you head north towards the parish of **St Andrew**, however, the land rises in a short series of peaks to the island's highest point, Mount Hillaby.

Despite its small area, central Barbados offers a considerable number of attractions to lure you away from the beach. The parish of St George has a rewarding cluster of historic sights: the **parish church**, the military signal station at **Gun Hill**, and the beautiful plantation house at **Francia**. To the north in St Thomas – slap-bang in the middle of the island – is **Harrison's Cave**, a series of weirdly beautiful subterranean chambers. The narrow strip of jungle at nearby **Welchman Hall Gully**, hemmed in by cliffs and densely covered with the island's most attractive plants and trees, offers a unique glimpse of the island in its primal state, while the gardens at **Flower Forest** offer a more carefully managed look at local flora.

Further north, you can drive to the top of **Mount Hillaby** for a view over the rugged landscape of the Scotland district, or evade the tourists completely by walking through the virgin forest at **Turner's Hall Woods,** little-disturbed since the island was first visited by Europeans.

Getting there and getting around

Getting to and around the interior of Barbados is straightforward – buses from Bridgetown (see p.39) run to the main attractions, though services are less frequent than on the coasts. You'll save a lot of time (and do a lot more exploring) if you rent a car for a day or two – a network of country lanes criss-cross the centre, offering easy access from the coast (see p.17 for a list of rental agencies).

....

Surprisingly, given the area's natural beauty, there's still nowhere to stay in central Barbados, and eating options are strictly limited. It's only a short journey, though, from either the west or south coasts, with their plethora of hotels and restaurants.

....

ST GEORGE'S PARISH CHURCH

Map 2, C7. Daily 9am–4pm; free.

Just north of Highway 4, the picturesque **St George's Parish Church** was originally built in the 1630s, just a decade after the British first settled in Barbados. Like all of the island's old wooden churches, it was destroyed in the ferocious hurricane of 1780; the present building dates from 1784 and, having withstood the hurricanes of 1831, 1898 and 1955, it's the oldest complete church in the country. With its Georgian arched windows and doors, and Gothic buttressing and battlements, the church is an odd architectural hybrid, but it's a pleasant, quiet spot to take a break from the heat of the day. The altar painting of the resurrection, *Rise to Power,* by Benjamin West, American president of the Royal Academy of Arts in London from 1792 to 1820, is one of the finest church paintings on the island.

Elsewhere, the church contains several fine marble commemorative sculptures made in England, including a tablet by Richard Westmacott, sculptor of the statues of Nelson in Trafalgar Square, London and Bridgetown (see p.41). There is also an attractive series of stained glass windows illustrating Biblical scenes in the airy chancel. Outside, the extensive cemetery, where old tombs crumble beneath various types of palm, offers a shady stroll and lovely views.

GUN HILL SIGNAL STATION

Map 2, C7. Mon–Sat 9am–5pm; B$9.20.

Less than two kilometres to the north of St George's Parish Church, **Gun Hill Signal Station** sits among pretty landscaped gardens that belie its turbulent origins (see box). Built in 1818 and impressively restored by the Barbados National Trust, the watchtower offers fabulous panoramic views across the green, gently rolling hills of central Barbados and out to the ocean beyond Bridgetown. Guides give an expert introduction to the local history, and there is a small but immaculate display of military memorabilia, including flags of the various army regiments that were stationed here, maps of the island's many forts – 23 of them

Signal Stations

Gun Hill was one of a chain of six **signal stations** that were quickly constructed on high ground across Barbados after the island's first and only mass slave revolt in 1816 (see p.75). In the era before the telephone, semaphore flags and lanterns were the fastest means of communication over long distances. The stations could rapidly pass signals between the east and west coasts; within minutes of trouble in even the remotest part of the island, the garrison in Bridgetown could put be on alert, or have soldiers marching out to quell any trouble.

The stations were also on standby to warn of the arrival of enemy shipping, though in the event neither domestic revolt nor enemy invasion took place, and the semaphore signals were only ever used to advise of the safe arrival of cargo and passenger ships. With the introduction of telephone, the stations became unnecessary, and were abandoned in 1887.

Two other signal stations survive on Barbados: the Cotton Tower in St Joseph (see p.119) and Grenade Hall in the north of the island (see p.102).

had been built as early as 1728 – and the cannons (never fired) that would have alerted the population of enemy invasion. Below the station, and visible from the tower, is a giant **white lion** – a British military emblem carved from a single block of limestone by soldiers stationed here in 1868.

FRANCIA

Map 2, C7. Mon–Fri 10am–4pm; B$9.

Just south of Gun Hill, signposted off to the west, is **Francia**, a working plantation growing sweet potatoes, yams and eddoes for export. The plantation house is one of the most attractive in Barbados; it was also one of the last of the island's great houses, built at the turn of the twentieth century when the plantations were already in decline as the value of sugar fell on world markets. The sweeping stone staircase, triple-arched entrance and enclosed upper balcony are unusual features, reflecting the influence of the French owner. The double-jalousied windows are also rare on Barbados, though they are also found at the nineteenth-century Tyrol Cot in Bridgetown (see p.50).

The pride of the house – and what really distinguishes it from the other great houses you can tour – is its superb collection of **antique maps** of Barbados and the Caribbean, collected from dusty bookshops and grand auction rooms around the world and dating back to the early sixteenth century, only decades after Columbus first "discovered" the region. A spectacular chandelier hangs over the dining table, and there's the usual array of mahogany furniture, much of it predating the house itself, including a three-seater nineteenth-century love-seat (for lovers and their chaperones). Outside, the huge terraced garden feels very English in style, despite the abundance of tropical flora including a gigantic mammee apple tree, mangoes, frangipani, hibiscus and the ubiquitous bougainvillea. The stack of round coral dripstones was used to filter rainwater to make it drinkable in the days before piped water.

HARRISON'S CAVE

Map 2, C6. 40-min tours daily 9am–4pm; B$17.25.

Fifteen minutes' drive north of Francia Plantation, **Harrison's Cave** is an enormous subterranean labyrinth, where underground streams and dripping water have carved huge limestone caverns with stalactites hanging like teeth from the ceilings and weirdly shaped stalagmites pushing up from the cave floor. The existence of caves here has been known for over two hundred years, though it was only by accident that the caves you'll see on your tour were discovered in 1970, and subsequently opened up to the public.

No serious potholing is expected of you – you're taken underground and around the various chambers on an electric tram, which, with the guide's mechanical voice-over, rather spoils the eerie, otherwise soundless atmosphere of the place. However, it can't completely detract from the beauty – you'll be hard put to find more spectacular cave scenery anywhere in the world. A twelve-metre waterfall plunges into one of the smaller caves, a river pours silently through another, while, in a third, a huge icy green lake offers a unusual swimming opportunity if you've got the nerve. Sit at the back of the tram with one of the guards, and ask them to point out some of the great shapes made by the dripping limestone: the pope, a mother and child, and a flock of vultures. As usual, there's a small gift shop and a snack bar once you've finished the tour.

WELCHMAN HALL GULLY

Map 2, C6. Mon–Sat 9am–5pm; B$11.50.

A kilometre or so north of Harrison's Cave, the dramatic **Welchman Hall Gully** is a long, deep corridor of jungle, hemmed in by steep cliffs and abounding with local flora and fauna. Though a handful of non-indigenous plants have been planted here over the years, the vegetation is not dissimilar to that which covered the whole island when the British first arrived here. The gully itself was created eons ago by a fissure in the limestone cap that covers this part of Barbados, and is named after a Welshman, General

Williams, an early settler on the island and the first owner of the surrounding land. There are two entrances – one at either end of the gully and both with parking spaces – and buses from Bridgetown stop outside each one.

A footpath leads down into the gully, and it's a little over a kilometre's walk from one end of the marked trail to the other. Prolific fruit and spice trees dangling with lianas offer protection from the sun; test your botanical knowledge as you walk by looking out for nutmeg, clove and fig trees, as well as the numerous ginger lilies, ferns and palms.

> **Keep an eye out for green monkeys (see p.102), which can be spotted playing around in the undergrowth of Welchman Hall Gully in the early morning or late afternoon.**

THE FLOWER FOREST

Map 2, C5. Daily 9am–5pm; B$12.

As you head across the parish boundary into St Joseph, the immaculately landscaped **Flower Forest** is signposted just south of Highway 2. There is a great variety of indigenous and imported plants and trees here, all labelled with their Latin and English names and country of origin, and some fabulous views over the hills of the Scotland district, but overall the place feels just a little bit too neat and ordered. If you only have timeto visit one of the island's botanical gardens, you're probably better off making for the more rugged Andromeda Gardens on the east coast (see p.120), but the Flower Forest is certainly worth a look if you're in the area.

The "forest" is on the site of the old Richmond sugar plantation, converted in the 1980s into a tourist attraction, with imported flowers, trees and shrubs planted and indigenous ones encouraged to proliferate across the former sugar fields. A path runs around the borders, divided into sections coyly (and rather unnecessarily) named "Don's Downhill", "Colin's Corner" and "Mary's Meadow", and it'll take you thirty to forty minutes to complete the circuit. The list of trees is almost endless, including breadfruit, coffee, Barbados cherry, avocado, and a single, African baobab tree, and there is a fine collection of orchids, hibiscus and the 'lobster claw' heliconias. Other highlights include Palm Walk, where dozens of different types of palm are scattered around, making a pleasant, shady place to cool off with a picnic and a good book.

MOUNT HILLABY

Map 2, C5.

Back on Highway 2, a brief detour will take you to **Mount Hillaby**, at 335m the highest point on Barbados, with suitably commanding views of the island. Make a left turn at Baxters – a sharp uphill beside a faded pink chattel house – and follow the road, covered in road tennis markings, straight through to the pretty little village of Hillaby. Turn left by the church (past the mini-mart) and follow the road for over a kilometre to the very top, where you can park. From here, you can look out over the Atlantic-lashed east coast, or take the grassy and sometimes overgrown path on the right that leads to the summit and more panoramic views.

TURNER'S HALL WOODS

Map 2, C5.

Just north of Mount Hillaby, though a little awkward to

get to, **Turner's Hall Woods** is the last area of Barbados still covered in the primary rainforest that the first settlers encountered when they landed on the island. As soon as you set foot in the woods, the humidity makes you aware that you have entered a radically different ecosystem. Although there's no particular target to make for, you can follow the track (once a proper road) that leads through the centre of the woods. This is a fascinating and atmospheric place to wander, surrounded by ancient vegetation – lianas, mahogany trees and some magnificent silk cotton trees.

To get to Turner's Hall, take the signposted left off Highway 2 to St Simons soon after you pass Haggatts government agriculture station (a right leads to the potteries at Chalky Mount – see below). Follow the sideroad through the small rural village and right to the end of the track, where you can park a hundred metres from the entrance to the woods. If you're coming by bus, look for the St Simons or Shorey bus from Bridgetown.

CHALKY MOUNT

Map 2, C5.

Signposted to the right off Highway 2, **Chalky Mount** is the highest peak on a range of hills famous for its soil, whose reddish-brown colour betrays it as the island's main source of clay. Potters have operated in the area for generations, and the small village of Chalky Mount – a short hike from the summit – still features a handful of them. Handpainted signs point you to several factories where you can see the clay workers in action, each with an attached shopselling sensibly priced mugs, pots and "monkey jugs", traditionally used for keeping drinking water cool.

THE NORTH

The **north of Barbados** is the most rugged and least visited part of the island, but nonetheless offers an excellent variety of places to explore. The most popular target is the **Barbados Wildlife Reserve**, home to hundreds of green monkeys and a host of other animals; nearby, there's an old signal station and a nature trail through the forest at **Grenade Hall**, while the lovely park and desolate ruins at **Farley Hill** make a good place to stop for a picnic. Just north of here there is a working **sugar mill** at Morgan Lewis and a superb Jacobean great house, **St Nicholas Abbey**. Further north still, the parish of **St Lucy** offers dramatic scenery, particularly at **Cove Bay**, another great picnic spot, and exotic marine life at **Animal Flower Cave**, right on the island's northern tip.

Getting there and getting around

Buses run through the northern parishes from both Speightstown and Bridgetown, though services are less regular than along the south and west coasts. If you're planning on visiting more than one of the main attractions – and you could comfortably see all of them in a day – renting a car will make getting around a lot less hassle.

There are no hotels in the northern tip of the
island – the nearest are around Speightstown
(see p.140).

BARBADOS WILDLIFE RESERVE

Map 2, C4. Daily 9am–5pm; B$23 (including access to Grenade
Hall).

Green monkeys are the chief attraction at the **Barbados
Wildlife Reserve**, just off Highway 1 in the parish of St
Peter and directly accessible by bus from Speightstown or
Bridgetown. The non-profitmaking reserve was first established as the island's leading centre for conservation of the
monkeys (see box), and – more controversially – to look at
the possibility of exporting them for medical research, particularly the production and testing of vaccines. As the idea
of making it into a tourist attraction developed, other creatures were gradually introduced, including brocket deer,
who normally hide shyly in the undergrowth, otters,
armadillos, raccoons and caiman alligators, as well as plenty
of caged parrots, macaws and other fabulously coloured
tropical birds.

Paths meander through the lush mahogany woods and, in
a thirty-minute stroll, you'll see pretty much everything on
offer – the aviary, fishponds, birdcages and plenty of animals. The monkeys are the highlight, swarming freely
around the reserve in playful mood. You can sometimes see
them making a break for the outside, leaping from trees
over the perimeter fence; apparently, they always return.
Don't try to get too close – they can inflict a nasty bite if
provoked – and bear in mind that they are not averse to
snatching any cameras or bags left in an accessible place.

BARBADOS WILDLIFE RESERVE

Green Monkeys

Green monkeys first came to Barbados from West Africa around 1650, almost certainly as pets of the slave traders on one of the early ships. They soon established a firm foothold in the island's woods and gullies and, though they haven't spread to the surrounding West Indies, they remain prolific on Barbados. They're pretty shy creatures, but you've a good chance of seeing one (or even a troupe) of the estimated five thousand loping across a road as you drive around the interior.

Predictably, and to the fury of local farmers, the monkeys have a liking for many of the island's crops; as a result, a bounty has been offered on their heads (or tails) since 1679. Nowadays, the Primate Research Centre at the Wildlife Reserve (see p.101) offers a more substantial inducement if they are delivered alive, so you may see monkey traps scattered around – usually nothing more complex than a banana in a cage.

There is plenty of island folklore about the green monkeys, perhaps most endearingly that – like their human cousins – they bury their dead. Modern zoologists scoff at such suggestions but will, if pressed, admit that skeletons are rarely found.

Don't miss the **information centre**, at the northeast corner of the reserve, which has excellent displays on the monkeys as well as a handful of rather sad-looking snakes.

GRENADE HALL SIGNAL STATION AND FOREST

Map 2, C4. Daily 9am–5pm; B\$23 (including access to Wildlife Reserve).

The **Grenade Hall Signal Station** was one of the chain of communication stations built in the years immediately after Barbados faced its first and only major slave revolt in 1816 (see p.75). The stations, which communicated by semaphore flags and lanterns, were designed to get news of any trouble afoot rapidly to the garrison in Bridgetown.

Grenade Hall is not as attractively located as Gun Hill (see p.93), though the watchtower offers great views of the surrounding countryside, and the place is certainly worth a quick tour if you're in the area. Prints of the British military hang downstairs, alongside various bits and pieces belonging to the signalmen and found in the ruins during restoration – medallions, clay pipes, coins and pottery shards. Upstairs, the old semaphore signals are on display – though most of them postdate the era of possible slave revolts, and relate to shipping movements. There is an old-fashioned telephone and a brief display on the invention that made the signal stations obsolete.

Below Grenade Hall, a large tract of **native forest** (same hours and ticket) has been preserved, and several kilometres of pathways loop down through the woods and under whitewood, dogwood, mahogany and magnificent silk cotton trees. Walking down from the signal station you can feel yourself entering a different eco-system – shaded, damp, humid and sticky – and the network of paths is complex enough to make it easy to get lost (albeit briefly). Boards have been put up along the trail, listing the names and medicinal values of some of the plants and trees and, back at the entrance, there's a detailed description of traditional "bush medicine".

FARLEY HILL NATIONAL PARK

Map 2, C4. Daily 8am–6pm; free; car B$5.

Just south of the wildlife reserve, **Farley Hill National Park** is a small, pleasant park at the top of a 300-metre cliff, with commanding views over the Scotland district (see p.118). It's a good place to retreat with a picnic once you've finished looking around Grenade Hall. The park is also the site of what was once a spectacular great house, built for a sugar baron in the early nineteenth century and opulently restored in 1956 when it was used as the setting for the movie *Island in the Sun*, starring Harry Belafonte. Hollywood descended in force, adding an immaculate new gallery, staircase and open veranda, painting trees to get the 'right' colour of leaf, and pumping colossal amounts of precious water into the leaky artificial lake.

The movie was a reasonable success, but – possibly because of the inflammable materials added to the mansion – the place went up in flames a few years later, leaving the old house completely gutted. No attempt was made to repair the damage and in 1965 the government bought the land and converted it into a park, officially opened by Queen Elizabeth a year later. Today, the charred coral block walls of the rather ghostly mansion form the park's focus, surrounded by landscaped lawns and masses of fruit trees.

MORGAN LEWIS SUGAR MILL

Map 2, C4. Daily 9am–4.30pm; B$10.

Set in the midst of the crumbling ruins of an old sugar factory, a tall chimney poking defiantly from the overgrown grass, **Morgan Lewis Sugar Mill** is the only windmill in Barbados that's still in operation. The island once boasted more than five hundred mills, all grinding juice from the sugarcane that covered the island like a blanket, but twentieth-century mechanization has all but eliminated them from the countryside. The Morgan Lewis mill, if not an essential object of pilgrimage during your stay on Barbados, provides an attractive and atmospheric testament to this part of the island's history.

Though it's no longer in commercial use, the mill – first built in the nineteenth century – is still in perfect working order. The sails, wheelhouse and British-made machinery have been thoroughly restored over the last few years, and you'll get a demonstration of how the thick bamboo-like stems were pushed through mechanical grinders to extract cane juice, subsequently used for making sugar. There's also a small display on the history of the mills.

MORGAN LEWIS BEACH

Map 2, C4.

A short drive away, **Morgan Lewis Beach** is one of the most remote spots on the island; given the strong undercurrents, swimming here is highly dangerous. Head uphill, then turn onto a narrow road for a kilometre until you reach the first houses of **Boscobelle**, where you turn sharply right down a rutted but passable track which eventually leads to the grassy, windblown slopes above the beach. There's rarely anyone around this untamed area and no houses in sight, and it's a decent place to chill out for an hour or two before you continue touring.

CHERRY TREE HILL

Map 2, C3.

Continuing north uphill, the main road sweeps past the sugar fields before reaching a magnificent canopy of mahogany trees at **Cherry Tree Hill**, and it's worth stopping to look behind you across the east coast and out to the Atlantic Ocean – one of the most spectacular views on the island. There is actually no record of cherry trees having existed here; the local legend that they were all chopped down because passers-by kept stealing the fruit sounds a little unlikely.

ST NICHOLAS ABBEY

Map 2, C3. Mon–Fri 10am–3.30pm; B$10.

Over the brow of the hill, a right turn takes you to the great house of **St Nicholas Abbey** – the oldest house on Barbados and one of only three Jacobean plantation houses left standing in all of the Americas (the others are the privately-owned Drax Hall and a castle in Virginia, USA).

Built during the 1650s, the white-painted house with its distinctive ogee gables was originally owned by two of the largest sugar-growers in the north of the island. The name St Nicholas, however, came about much later, on account of the house's early nineteenth-century owners who hailed from St Nicholas parish in Bristol, England. How the place came to be called an abbey, though, is unclear. So too is the reason for the fireplaces – completely unnecessary in view of the island's tropical weather – in the upstairs bedrooms. Presumably they are the result of the builders' slavishly following the drawings of a British architect, regardless of the Caribbean climate.

Your entrance fee gets you a rather lacklustre guided tour of the ground floor of the house (the upstairs is still used, and closed to visitors), crammed with eighteenth-century furniture, Wedgwood porcelain and other traditional accoutrements of the old Barbadian aristocracy; the outbuildings at the back of the house are rather more rustic, and include the original bath house and a four-seater toilet.

The tour of the house may be a little unexciting, but – if you time it right – there is one unmissable highlight, an evocative twenty-minute black-and-white **film** that is shown in the old stables daily at 11.30am and 2.30pm. Made in 1934 by a previous owner of the abbey (with a languid voice-over by the present owner) it shows the family making a visit by sea from England to their West Indian home. There is some great footage of the boats arriving at Bridgetown harbour and of the pre-war city, with its horse-drawn carts and early cars, followed by loving shots of the sugar plantation in action, with the kids playing their dangerous game of hanging onto one of the sails of the windmill until it had completed a dizzying circle. Once you've seen the film, you can take a short stroll through the woods behind the house or grab a drink in the small café.

COVE BAY

Map 2, C3.

Heading northeast from St Nicholas Abbey into the parish of St Lucy, **Cove Bay** is the first – and one of the most beautiful – of a series of coves carved into the island's north coast by the lashing Atlantic surf. Head through Cave Hill to Pie Corner – where a signposted right turn takes you out to the bay, past a small horse-riding stables and an old, crumbling windmill and across a grassy field. There is a small, stony beach that you can clamber down to if you're desperate to swim, but the water is rough and rocky and you'll probably want to wait until you're somewhere calmer.

Much more appealing is the view – elegant rows of palm trees stand just above the water's edge, buffeted by the always fresh trade winds, and you can see down the entire length of the east coast. On your right, a white cliff rises up to a sharp point 76m above the sea, rather grandly known as Pico Tenerife.

As Cove Bay has grown in appeal, a handful of local hustlers have started hanging out en route to the bay, trying to flag down cars and offering their assistance in finding the place in return for an unspecified tip. You'll probably want to decline their services – the bay isn't hard to find, and if you are feeling lost, you'd be better off asking someone who isn't so blatantly after a tip.

LITTLE BAY

Map 2, C3.

A turning on the left shortly before you reach Cove Bay, **Little Bay** is another rocky, foam-sprayed spot where the surf has carved caves, tunnels and arches into the cliffs. Again, it's not a great place to swim, but at low tide there are plenty of rockpools to explore and you can clamber out to look around the caves. Leatherback turtles occasionally crawl onto the beach here to bury their eggs, though your chances of seeing them or their trails are pretty remote.

RIVER BAY

Map 2, C3.

From Little Bay you can pick your way a couple of kilometres along the coast to **River Bay**, which gets its name from a stream that runs out to the sea through a small, steep-sided valley. It's a popular weekend spot with Bajans, who drive down here for a picnic, and when the water is high it's a pleasant enough place to swim.

ANIMAL FLOWER CAVE

Map 2, B3. Daily 10am–4pm; B$6.

Right at the barren, rocky northern tip of the island, the rather spooky **Animal Flower Cave** has been a tourist attraction for centuries. Created by the battering of thousands of years of Atlantic waves, the cave is still out of bounds when the sea is rough, and you may want to call ahead (©439 8797) if you're dubious about the weather.

A guide takes you into the cave, clambering down some stairs and across a slippery floor overhung with stalactites and filled with sinkholes and rockpools, in which dozens of tiny but colourful sea anemones and filter-feeding tube worms (the "animal flowers") wave their little tentacles about. Early visitors like English churchman Griffith Hughes collected the "flowers" in the 1740s, taking specimens home to supply mini-museums. Though the numbers of the "flowers" have been heavily depleted since Hughes's day, it remains an eerie and evocative place.

ARCHER'S BAY

Map 2, B3.

West of Animal Flower Cave, a rocky path leads down to a small sandy beach at **Archer's Bay** – a popular local spot, signposted off the main highway, but again often too rough for swimming. Heading south from here, the road leads down to the unremarkable and usually locked St Lucy's Parish Church.

MAYCOCK'S BAY

Map 2, A3.

A better bet is to continue west, where a small branch off

Amerindians in Barbados

The north coast of Barbados is dotted with sites where archeological digs have shown the presence of sizeable **Amerindian settlements**. The Amerindians were the first known inhabitants of Barbados, arriving by dugout canoe from Venezuela and Guyana in several waves starting around 350 AD. These Arawak-speaking people had typical Mongoloid features, with straight black hair and dark eyes. In "middens" (rubbish dumps) across the island, they left enough of their tools and pottery to allow archeologists to build up a picture of their way of life.

They were primarily fishermen, as well as simple farmers, with most of their settlements set just back from the sea, often around swamp or marsh land that provided fresh water. Their staple food was cassava, supplemented by shellfish, fish and turtles (conch and turtle shells were shaped and used as tools). Variations in their pottery styles over succeeding centuries suggest that they continued to be influenced by contact with the people of Latin America, and may have traded with other Caribbean islands.

Though Columbus never visited Barbados, it is likely that there were still Amerindians living on the island during his late fifteenth-century exploration of the area. By 1536, however, sailors reported the island uninhabited. Spanish raids for slaves to toil in the gold and silver mines of Hispaniola were probably responsible, prompting Barbados's first people to flee to more secure hiding places on other islands or the South American mainland.

the main road (before you reach the turning for the cement plant) cuts down to the coast at lovely **Maycock's Bay**. This area is the site of **Maycock's Fort**, one of the island's principal defences in the seventeenth century. It was built in 1638, just north of a small river inlet, to protect against enemy incursion. Sadly, the fort's ancient coral stone walls and powder magazines are now almost completely ruined, and few people make the effort to reach it. If you're interested, it's just a short stroll down from the end of the paved track.

SIX MEN'S BAY

Map 2, A4.

Below Maycock's Bay, the main road swings back alongside the coast and passes through a series of small, quiet fishing villages; perhaps the most picturesque of these is the former whaling port of **Six Men's Bay**, where colourfully painted fishing boats line the shore. Continue south past the spectacular new development of **Port St Charles** marina, where luxury apartments with their own yachting berth change hands for millions of dollars, and the highway will take you back into Speightstown (see p.87).

THE EAST COAST

For many people, the rugged, little-explored east coast is the most beautiful part of Barbados. Almost all year round, the Atlantic waves crash in against this wild and spectacular coastline, making swimming difficult and dangerous – though the surfing is superb. It's certainly worth making the effort to explore a different side of the island from the heavily tourism south and west; if possible, try to spend a night or two up here. If you can't stay, do at least check out one of the excellent restaurants around the laid-back old resort of **Bathsheba** for lunch.

For details of east coast accommodation, see p.141.

Although the coastal scenery is the main attraction, there are a few specific places that merit a visit as you pass through. **Andromeda Botanical Gardens** is a particularly delightful spot, while the centuries-old theological school at **Codrington College** and the historic **St John's Parish Church** are also worth a brief stop. But, specific sightseeing apart, this is a lovely area to drive through, particularly under the steep-sided **Hackleton's Cliff** that runs parallel to the coast, where the road weaves up and down through lush tropical forest, offering stunning views over

Railway days

The scenic, winding, modern road that takes you through the plantations and along the cliffs of Barbados's east coast is a recent phenomenon, built during the 1960s. Prior to this there were only rough, barely passable tracks, and this created major headaches for plantation owners, who faced a real challenge to get their hogsheads of sugar from the estates to the west coast ports for export. In the 1880s the British came up with a typical solution, carving the island's first and only **railway line** from Bridgetown, along the south coast and then up the east coast as far as Belleplaine.

As well as helping out the sugar growers, the new railway line boosted local tourism and encouraged Bajans to take holidays on their own east coast, particularly around Bathsheba, a habit that many families continue today. However, by the early twentieth century the track was already in serious disrepair, with sea erosion and landslides taking their toll – the scheduled three-hour journey could easily take up to twelve – and in 1937 the government finally called time on the trains.

the ocean, and you can walk for kilometres along the brown sandy beaches at **Bath** and **Martin's Bay**, watching the surf ride in.

RAGGED POINT

Map 2, G6.

Highway 5 runs east across Barbados from Bridgetown, ending up at the easternmost end of the island near **Ragged Point**. This is one of the wildest and most isolated spots on Barbados, where Atlantic breakers pound the limestone cliffs. The East Point Lighthouse stands on a peninsula nearby; though now disused, it is one of the main landmarks on this side of the island, providing dramatic views up the coast.

Lashed by the Atlantic surf, the waters of the island's east coast can be treacherous for swimmers, with dangerous currents and riptides frequently pulling people to their death. Bath is one of the few safe spots; elsewhere, watch the locals – if they're swimming you can usually assume it's okay to go in, but watch your depth and never go in on your own.

CODRINGTON COLLEGE

Map 2, F6. Daily 10am–4pm; B$5.

Signposted on your right as you head up the east coast, Skeete Bay and Consett Bay are a couple of quiet, pretty coves, each with a strip of sand backed by palm trees and with fishing boats pulled up on the beach. Just north of Consett Bay, on the clifftop, stand the handsome buildings of **Codrington College**. The first degree-level institution in the English-speaking West Indies, it continues to teach theology to budding Anglican vicars, and is now affiliated to the University of the West Indies.

The approach to the college is dramatic, along a long avenue lined on either side with a graceful row of tall cabbage palms and ending beside a large ornamental lake covered in waterlilies. The buildings are arranged around an unfinished quadrangle, with an arched central portico which opens onto large, elegant gardens offering panoramic views over the coast. The modest chapel is on your right as you enter, and the main hall, carrying a bust of

Christopher Codrington

Christopher Codrington was a wealthy Barbadian landowner in the later seventeenth century and Governor of the Leeward Islands from 1698 to 1702. At his death in 1710, he bequeathed the wealth of his sugar plantations for the foundation of a Christian training college. Because his family contested the will, it took decades for his wish to be implemented, and the college was only established in 1748.

Codrington, on your left. The principal's lodge, on the west side of the college, was the original seventeenth-century great house of the sugar plantation and, though damaged by fire and hurricane, parts of the original still remain, including the coral stone porch and some of the carved Jacobean balustrades. A stone's throw to the west, a short nature trail has been laid out through the woods – a gentle place to wander for fifteen minutes or so.

BATH AND MARTIN'S BAY

Map 2, F6.

Continuing north from the college, the tall, overgrown chimney of the ruined Bath sugar factory marks the turn-off to **Bath**. This curved brown sand beach is one of the safest places to swim on the east coast, backed by thick groves of casuarina trees and protected offshore by a long stretch of coral reef which is ideal for snorkelling. There's a children's play area, picnic tables by the water and, on weekends and holidays, a steady stream of Bajans coming to splash around and play beach cricket.

Back on the main road, you'll pass the giant satellite dish that keeps the island in touch with the outside world. The

Hiking on the east coast

It's possible to walk along great lengths of the eastern coast-line, between Skeete's Bay in St Philip and Barclays Park in St Joseph, alternating between beach, paved road and parts of the disused railway line. You'll find few tourists about, and can expect to see plenty of fishing boats, seabirds and even the odd osprey. One of the best walks is between Martin's Bay and Bath, most of it following a trail along an old railway right-of-way, though at one point you'll have to cut inland around an abandoned railway bridge. Alternatively, wander between Bathsheba and Cattlewash, either along the beach or the old railway track; en route, you'll cross Joe's River – one of just two permanently flowing rivers in Barbados – and can cut inland to look at the dense woods that border it, before stopping for a bite to eat at the *Kingsley Club* or *Edgewater Hotel* (see p.162).

road weaves in and out of the coast, past large sugar and banana plantations, en route to the small fishing village of **Martin's Bay**, which nestles on the coast beneath Hackleton's Cliff (see below). The village makes an ideal starting point for a hiking tour of the coast (see box).

ST JOHN'S PARISH CHURCH

Map 2, E6. Daily 9am–5pm; free.

From Martin's Bay, a steep road climbs dramatically up through Hackleton's Cliff. Turn left at the top of the hill, past more sweeping fields of sugarcane, for the Gothic **St John's Parish Church**, probably the most elegant of the island's churches. Like many of the parish churches, St John's – typically English with its arched doors and windows and graceful tower – was first built in the mid-seventeenth century but, following severe hurricane damage in the great storm of 1831, now dates from around 1836.

The floor of the church is paved with ancient memorial tablets, rescued from earlier versions of the building, and a Madonna and child sculpture by Richard Westmacott stands to the left of the main entrance. Most attractive of all is the reddish-brown pulpit, superbly hand-carved from four local woods (mahogany, ebony, manchineel and locust) and imported oak and pine. Outside, the expansive graveyard is perched on top of the cliff, looking down over miles of

Last of the Byzantines

One of the oldest tombs in the St John's graveyard is that of **Ferdinand Paleologus**, thought to have been the final surviving descendant of the brother of Constantine XI – the last emperor of the Byzantine Greeks – who was killed in battle when present-day Istanbul was captured by the Turks in 1453. Ferdinand's family moved to England, where he was brought up, and he fought for King Charles I during the English Civil War. Like many defeated Royalists, he fled to Barbados in 1646, where he became a churchwarden of St John's and, later, a lieutenant in the militia.

Ferdinand's coffin was discovered in a vault during restoration work after the 1831 hurricane, facing in the opposite direction to the other coffins (with the head pointing west) and with the large skeleton embedded in quicklime, both customs of the Greek Orthodox Church. During the Greek War of Independence of the 1820s, the provisional Greek government made enquiries in Barbados to see if there was any surviving male descendant of Ferdinand still alive who might return as a figurehead for their new battle with the Turks. None was found.

jagged coastline and crammed with moss-covered tombs, family vaults and a wide array of tropical flora.

HACKLETON'S CLIFF AND SCOTLAND

Map 2, D6.
From the church, follow the road north where, after a kilometre or so, a sign diverts you to **Hackleton's Cliff**. This steep 300m limestone escarpment marks the edge of the **Scotland** district to the west and, to the east, the rugged east coast whose limestone cap was eroded by sea action many centuries ago. At the end of a short track, you can park right by the edge of the cliff, for fabulous views across the craggy hills of Scotland, nostalgically named by early settlers for its supposed resemblance to the land of Robert Burns, and up the sandy northeast coastline. It's a peaceful spot, where the only sound is often the calling of the swifts as they wheel away on the warm currents of air rising from the ground hundreds of metres below.

VILLA NOVA

Map 2, D6.
North of the cliff, a left-hand turn leads down to **Villa Nova**, one of the most famous of the island's sugar plantation great houses, currently under consideration for conversion into a Swiss-owned luxury hotel. The new house ("villa nova") dates from 1833, after its predecessor was destroyed by the 1831 hurricane. Many of the island's leading dignitaries lived here, and former British prime minister Anthony Eden owned it for a while in the 1960s, entertaining Queen Elizabeth II here during her visit in 1966. Sadly, the cost of upkeep defeated the last owners,

and the place is presently abandoned and in rather woeful condition.

You are free to wander around the grounds, through the gloomy approach road festooned with creepers dangling from the giant mahogany trees and onto the extensive, manicured lawns that teem with bird and butterfly life. The two-storied house is small but extremely attractive, with steps leading up to the wide, columned south porch and cool verandas spreading off to the sides, with a semi-circular parapet above the entrance to protect against storms. Inside, the once elegant ballroom whose wooden floor used to sound with the footsteps of waltz and polka dancers, is presently rotting under the effect of years of intrusive rain-water. Talk of restoration is undoubtedly timely; whether a five-star hotel will help retain the atmosphere of the place is another matter.

THE COTTON TOWER

Map 2, D6.

Back on the main road, you'll pass through the tiny village of Easy Hall and continue past the derelict remains of Buckden Great House, overgrown and rather eerie with the plants having pushed their way up through the floorboards and green monkeys scampering around on the delapidated roof. On your left, the pink **Cotton Tower** is one of the six signal stations built in the early nineteenth century to warn of slave uprisings or the arrival of enemy boats (see Gun Hill, p.93). This one, built in 1819 and named after Lady Caroline Cotton, daughter of the island's governor, is due for renovation and may be reopened to the public in 1999.

From the Cotton Tower, the road plunges steeply down-hill, past the unremarkable St Joseph's Parish Church, to the coast at Bathsheba (see p.122).

THE COTTON TOWER

Redlegs

Among the earliest settlers in Barbados were many – the flot-
sam and jetsam of seventeenth-century England and Scotland
– who came because they had little or no choice. This included
political and religious refugees, criminals sentenced to trans-
portation and impoverished servants who, in return for their
passage to the island, were obliged to work on the plantations
– without wages – for up to seven years. Those who survived
this indenture and remained on the island became a marginal-
ized group within Barbadian society, fitting into neither the
white planter class nor the growing ranks of Africans who
replaced them on the plantations. Whole communities of poor
white peasant farmers became established on the island's least
fertile land, particularly "below the hill" around Hackleton's
Cliff, inter-marrying and neglected by the authorities.

With the rapid social change of the last century, many of
these "redlegs" – so known for the effect of the sun on those
who wore kilts – have gradually become more integrated into
the community, with increased education opportunities leading
to profitable employment or a socially climbing marriage.
Nevertheless, there are still pockets in the middle of the general population where you'll find a chattel house holding a family
of poor whites, still scraping a living from the soil as their
ancestors have done for the past three centuries, and for all
the world as Bajan as their Afro-Barbadian neighbours.

ANDROMEDA BOTANICAL GARDENS

Map 2, D6. Daily 9am–5pm; B\$12.

The colourful, sprawling **Andromeda Botanical
Gardens** make up one of the most attractive spots on the

island, spread over a hillside strewn with coral boulders and offering fabulous vistas over the Bathsheba coastline. Created by local botanist Iris Bannochie in 1954, the gardens feature masses of local and imported shrubs and plants, landscaped around a trail that incorporates several ponds and a giant, ancient bearded fig tree.

The hibiscus garden, on your left as you enter, features every shade of hibiscus (even a grey hybrid), and is the best place to see the tiny humming-birds that frequent the place. The trail then takes you past some old traveller's trees and a small clump of papyrus before turning uphill past a series of brightly coloured heliconia – including the bizarrely shaped 'beefsteak' heliconia – and a panama hat tree. The bearded fig tree is the real star of the gardens, but there are plenty of other highlights, including a bank of frangipani, rose of Sharon trees, superb cycads and a *Bombax ellipticum*, also known as the shaving brush tree for the large pink-bristled flower it produces. At the lower end of the trail, the Queen Ingrid Palm Garden features dozens of types of palm, including the massive tailpot, largest of the fan palms and often used abroad for thatched roofing.

Local botanists offer an entertaining, free guided tour of the gardens each Wednesday at 10.30am. The *Hibiscus Café*, inside the garden, serves cutters, rotis and other snacks as well as delicious Barbadian cherry juice, and there's a small Best of Barbados gift shop with prints, T-shirts, books and bottles of rum.

Beyond the gardens the road continues down to the seafront and the *Atlantis Hotel* (see p.141), a slightly faded and very easygoing place overlooking **Tent Bay**, often lined with the boats of the local fishing fleet. Built in the 1880s, this was one of the first hotels to be put up outside Bridgetown and, though there's not a great deal to do, the place offers an excellent buffet lunch and is a good place to

ANDROMEDA BOTANICAL GARDENS

chill out with a drink or a book and maybe take a stroll up the beach.

BATHSHEBA

Map 2, D5.

A kilometre or so north of Andromeda you'll reach a cross-roads; the east coast road continues straight on, a left takes you towards Hackleton's Cliff (see p.118), while a right drops you down into **Bathsheba**. Picturesque, easygoing and washed by Atlantic breezes, this has long been a favoured resort for Bajans, with small holiday homes lining the roadside, though surprisingly few tourists make it up here.

If the bay here looks familiar, it's because this is one of the most painted landscapes in Barbados. Also known as the soup bowl, because of the crashing surf that comes racing in here pretty much all year round, the area is popular with surfers who stage annual tournaments. Unfortunately, the currents mean that it's not a good place to swim, but the wide brown beach is attractive here and an old pathway runs north and south if you fancy a walk.

....

Surfboards can be rented from the
Round House Hotel **(see p.142).**

....

NORTH FROM BATHSHEBA

Above Bathsheba, the east coast road runs alongside the eastern edge of the Scotland district (see p.118) through **Cattlewash**, a tiny village that derives its name from the traditional practice of local farmers of driving their cows down to the sea here. Continuing north towards the

Morgan Lewis sugar mill and St Nicholas Abbey (see p.106), the road leads through **Barclays Park**, the small and wholly untouristed town of **Belleplaine** and the tiny village of **Shorey**, where the Conrad Hunte Sports Club (named after one of the greatest cricketers Barbados has produced) boasts perhaps the island's remotest cricket pitch, with the Atlantic Ocean glistening behind it.

For more information on cricket in Barbados, see p.201.

LISTINGS

ACCOMMODATION

With hotels stringing out virtually back-to-back both north and east of Bridgetown, there is no shortage of **accommodation** in Barbados. Heading up the **west coast** - traditionally the swankier side of the island - you'll find most of the pricier options, many of them concentrated around the lovely Paynes Bay or on either side of

Accommodation prices

Accommodation listed in this guide is graded on a scale from ① to ⑦. These categories show the cost per night of the cheapest double rooms in each establishment during the winter season (mid-December to mid-April). Almost everywhere has a significant difference between its winter and summer prices, so for many places we have given both categories, with the winter price first. Bear in mind that if you book for a week or more, particularly as part of a package, prices will normally be much lower.

① less than $30   ② $30–49
③ $50–69   ④ $70–99
⑤ $100–139   ⑥ $140–179
                ⑦ $180 or more

Holetown, but thinning out considerably as you continue north towards Speightstown. On the **south coast**, where the beaches are just as good, accommodation is much more reasonably priced, with plenty of good-value guesthouses, particularly around Worthing and St Lawrence Gap, and other places that cater specifically for a younger crowd, like the windsurfing hotels in Maxwell and Silver Sands.

Reflecting the tourist preference for the beaches and calm waters of the west and south, there are very few options elsewhere on the island. A handful of small, long-established hotels still do a light trade on the wild **east coast**, around Bathsheba and Cattlewash – great for those who want to escape the crowds – but, perhaps surprisingly, there is as yet nowhere to stay in the **centre** or **north** of the island.

For those interested in staying in a private home, a number of families offer bed and breakfast from aroumd $20 per person; branches of the Barbados Tourism Authority (see p.26) normally have lists, or you can contact Bajan Holidays Inc. in Bridgetown (© and fax 246 438 4043). The latter also regularly update lists of apartments available for rent. There are, however, no youth hostels on the island and camping is banned.

Unless otherwise stated, all places mentioned below are on the beach.

BRIDGETOWN

There is little reason to stay in **Bridgetown** and the city has only a handful of hotels, catering primarily for people with business dealings in the capital. Most of these places are in Aquatic Gap, east of town before you reach the Garrison area.

All-inclusives

The latest trend in hotel accommodation in the Caribbean has been towards **"all-inclusive" hotels**, and Barbados is no exception. The simple concept behind these places is that you pay a single price that covers your room, all meals and, normally, all drinks and watersports, so you can "leave your wallet at home". Heavily pushed by travel agents (who take a commission on the total price), the all-inclusives really took off in the troubled Jamaica of the 1980s, where many tourists were nervous about leaving their hotel compound at all. Their relevance to an island like Barbados is rather more questionable.

From the local point of view, the main problem with all-inclusives is their devastating effect on the independent sector. Local restaurants, bars and watersports operators lose custom because guests are tied to their hotel, reluctant to leave it and pay "twice" for food, drink or windsurfing. Nonetheless, the hordes of repeat visitors at places like *Escape* and *Almond Beach* are proof that all-inclusivity has undoubtedly caught on in Barbados.

If you are thinking of booking an all-inclusive, focus on what you specifically want out of it. *Almond Beach* and *Club Rockley*, for example, have several restaurants and bars, so you don't have to face the same menu every night; smaller places like *Escape* offer less variety, but a bit more space on the beach. Remember, too, that the allure of drinking seven types of "free" cocktail in a night or stuffing your face at the "free" buffet quickly fades, and if you want to get out and sample Barbados's myriad great restaurants and bars, you're better off steering clear of all-inclusives.

Barbados Hilton
Map 2, B8. Aquatic Gap, ☏426 0200, fax 436 8946.
Beach, several restaurants and good squash facilities. The grounds hold some of the oldest military sites on the island (see p.57). ⑦

Grand Barbados Beach Resort

Map 2, B8. Aquatic Gap, ©426 4000, fax 429 2400.

Large but impersonal seven-storey hotel with 133 rooms, a gym, sauna and massage facilities. The beach is okay, though there's a rather monstrous pier jutting off it that holds the hotel's restaurant. ⑥/⑤

Great Escape

Map 2, B8. 1st Avenue, Belleville, ©436 3554, no fax.

Small guesthouse in a wealthy suburb just east of town. The red and white chattel house building is attractive, though the rooms are pretty basic. It's nowhere near a beach, but makes a useful fallback in busy times – during England v. West Indies test matches, for example. ②

Island Inn Hotel

Map 2, B8. Aquatic Gap, ©436 6393, fax 437 8035.

This moderately attractive hotel was originally built as a rum store for the British army stationed nearby in 1804. With only 25 rooms, it's small for an all-inclusive, so don't expect much in the way of variety, though there's a tiny pool and the place is just a minute's walk from a reasonable beach. ⑦

THE SOUTH COAST

Between Bridgetown and Oistins on the island's south coast, a string of small resorts sit beside the main highway, each slightly different from the rest, with its own bars, restaurants and stores. **Rockley** has the fabulous **Accra Beach**, but is otherwise exremely bland; Worthing has more character, with another great beach and most of the budget guesthouses; while buzzing **St Lawrence Gap** has most of the nightlife and a great variety of places to eat and drink. East of Oistins the accommodation thins out, with a handful of places in **Silver Sands** that attract windsurfers and, beyond that, only two places in the quiet southeast where the surf is much rougher.

ROCKLEY

Abbeville Hotel
Map 4, C5. Rockley, ✆435 7924, fax 435 8502.
Friendly and easygoing little place, motel-like in design, with a small pool. The rooms are simple, but the setting, around a courtyard and huge bar, gives the place a welcoming feel. ②

Accra Beach Hotel
Map 4, C5. Rockley, ✆435 8920, fax 435 6794.
Large, smart hotel with 52 elegantly furnished rooms right on the island's busiest beach, with palm trees strewn around the gardens and a giant swimming pool. ⑤–⑥

Club Rockley Barbados
Map 4, C3. Rockley, ✆435 7880, fax 435 8015.
Popular all-inclusive village, ten minutes' walk (or a shuttle ride) from the beach, with four restaurants, several pools, good sports facilities and its own night club and golf course. The 150 rooms mean that there's a lot of people about, but the design, with clusters of buildings spread over a massive complex, helps prevent it feeling too crowded. ⑦

ROCKLEY

Riviera Beach Apartment Hotel
Map 4, C4. Rockley, ☏435 8970, fax 435 8954.

Forty-room hotel across the road from Accra Beach. Nothing fancy, but decent value for a place that's a stone's throw from spectacluar Accra Beach. All rooms have a-c and most have kitchenettes. ④/③

Crystal Waters Guesthouse
Map 4, E5. ☏435 7514, no fax.

Probably the pick of the local guesthouses – no frills, but a friendly and comfortable place, with hardwood floors, a TV lounge, a delightful veranda and a laid-back beachside bar. Excellent breakfasts, too. ②

Maraval Guesthouse
Map 4, E5. ☏435 7437, no fax.

Mostly European budget-travellers at this funky little place, a stone's throw from the beach.There's a communal kitchen and eating area, and the owner is as helpful as you'll find. ②

Sandy Beach Island Resort
Map 4, E5. ☏435 8000, fax 435 8053.

Big pink and white hotel with tennis courts, a curiously landscaped pool and regular nightly entertainment. The rooms aren't up to much, but the beach is so good you won't be spending a lot of time in them. ⑤/④

Shells Guesthouse
Map 4, E5. ☏435 7253, no fax.

Eight simple rooms in this friendly place, with a TV lounge and a pleasant bar/dining area. It's a quiet, low-key operation, and an ideal place to chill out for a few days. ②/①

Summer Home on Sea
Map 4, E5. ©435 7424, no fax.

Easygoing guesthouse right on the beach, with seven decent rooms, some with kitchenettes, and a regular sprinkling of European backpackers working their way around the Caribbean. ②/①

ST LAWRENCE GAP AND DOVER

Casuarina Beach Club
Map 4, H5. Dover, ©428 3600, fax 428 2122.

Big, popular and beautifully landscaped hotel, on the best beach in the area, with tennis courts, a reasonable pool and one of the finest collections of local art in the country. ⑥/④

Divi Southwinds
Map 4, G5. St Lawrence Gap, ©428 7181, fax 428 4674.

A bit of a sprawling monstrosity, and expensive, but worth a look for the beach. Try to avoid getting sucked into the relentless time-share sales pitch. ⑦/⑤

Dover Beach Hotel
Map 4, H5. Dover, ©428 8075, fax 428 2122.

Comfortable, easygoing place beside a decent beach. All the 39 rooms have a–c, some have kitchenettes, and there's a good-size pool. ④/③

ST LAWRENCE GAP AND DOVER |

Meridian Inn

Map 4, H5. Dover, ℂ428 4051.

Nothing fancy about this pink block of self-catering apartments, right at the end of the coast road, but good value. ③/②

Rio Guesthouse

Map 4, H4. St Lawrence Gap, ℂ and fax 428 1546.

Only seven rooms at this Swiss–German guesthouse, popular with European budget travellers, but they're a decent size and very reasonably priced. ②

MAXWELL

Kingsway Beach Apartments

Map 4, I4. ℂ428 820.

Ten rather basic but colourful rooms at the western end of the coast road, with one day free if you stay for a week. ②/①

Sea Breeze Beach Hotel

Map 4, H5. ℂ428 2825, fax 428 2872.

The pick of the hotels in the area, large and well-landscaped with two swimming pools, a gym and some outdoor jacuzzis by a delightful beach. ⑥/④

Windsurf Village

Map 4, I4. ℂ428 9095, fax 428 2872.

Small pink hotel just off the main road, with little in the way of luxury but popular with windsurfers. ③/②

MAXWELL

Long Beach Club
Map 2, E9. Long Beach, ©428 6890, fax 428 4957.
Pleasant spot and the only hotel on this stretch of beach, with a
pool and attractively furnished rooms, and popular with an
older crowd. A good place to escape the south coast crowd, but
it can feel a bit isolated. ④/③

Ocean Spray Apartments
Map 2, E9. Inch Marlow, ©428 5426, fax 428 9032.
Easygoing little place in a secluded spot just east of Silver
Sands, attracting a young crowd of surfers. There's nothing
fancy about the twenty rooms, but all of them have ocean
views, a balcony and a kitchen. ③/②

Pegwell Inn
Map 4, J4. Welchs (just west of Oistins), ©428 6150
Tiny guesthouse that's the cheapest place to stay in
Barbados. The four rooms all have fans and private
bathrooms and, though it's beside the main road and can be
a little noisy, it's only a five minute walk to the beach.
②/①

Roman Beach Apartments
Map 2, D9. Miami Beach, ©428 7635, fax 428 2510.
Fabulous bougainvillea dominates this little group of simple
apartments, popular with European gay couples, five
minutes' walk from Oistins and right by a secluded stretch of
beach. ②

Silver Rock Hotel

Map 2, E9. Silver Sands, ✆428 2866, fax 420 6982.

Three-storey pink and white block with 33 comfortable rooms, a pool and a crowd of surfers. There's a decent restaurant on site, and most rooms have kitchenettes. Studios ⑤/③, one-bedroom apartments ⑤/④

Silver Sands Resort

Map 2, E9. Silver Sands, ✆428 6001, fax 428 3758.

The only full-blown resort in the area, elegantly furnished with two restaurants, tennis courts, a large swimming pool and over a hundred air-conditioned rooms spread across 50,000 square metres of landscaped grounds. ⑤/③

THE SOUTHEAST

There are only two places to stay in the southeast, where you'll find the surf higher and the swimming harder. Both places have a lot of character, but can feel a bit isolated, especially in summer when they're quiet.

Crane Beach Hotel

Map 2, G8. ✆423 6220, fax 423 5343.

Small, beautifully designed hotel, in a stunning setting high above the beautiful Crane Bay. Here are nineteen spacious and atmospheric rooms, with local mahogany furniture and hardwood floors, and a "Roman"-style pool – though it's hardly any distance to the beach. ⑥/⑤

Sam Lord's Castle

Map 2, G7. ✆423 7350, fax 423 5918.

More mansion house than castle, with a handful (and the best) of the 280 rooms in the main house and the rest scattered around the attractively landscaped gardens. There are three swimming pools, as well as tennis courts and an exercise room, and some form of entertainment – from a steel band to karaoke – is laid on nightly. ⑦/⑥

THE WEST COAST

Although the west, or "platinum" coast of Barbados is renowned for its luxury hotels, several of which are ranked among the best in the Caribbean, there are a handful of cheaper places sandwiched between them. There's less of a "resort" feel than in the south, with hotels spaced out at more or less regualr intervals along the coast. Towards Speightstown in the north, though, options are fewer; if you're looking to escape the crowded beaches this is a good place to make for. There are no budget hotels, but Speightstown's unofficial tourist officer, Junior Clement at the *Fisherman's Pub* (see p.161), rents out fairly basic but comfortable **chattel houses** and **apartments** from $30 a night.

FROM PROSPECT TO PAYNES BAY

Angler Apartments
Map 5, C9. Derricks, © and fax 432 0817.
A dozen self-catering apartments in three small blocks shaded by mango and breadfruit trees and set back 200m from the highway just south of the *Coconut Creek Hotel*. No pretensions to luxury and some of the decor is highly tacky, but the fan-cooled rooms are comfortable enough (ask for one with a queen bed), the atmosphere relaxed and friendly, and you're five minutes' walk from a good beach. ④/③

THE WEST COAST

Beachcomber Apartments

Map 5, C8. Paynes Bay, ✆432 0489, fax 432 2824.

Small apartment block that's popular with families, offering large, luxurious, air-conditioned two-bedroom apartments – each with a huge balcony overlooking Paynes Bay – sleeping up to six for $370/$185 in winter/summer, and studios with smaller balconies sleeping two for $160/90. The larger rooms have full kitchens, the studios have small kitchenettes. ⑦

Chrizel's Guesthouse

Map 5, C10. ✆ and fax 438 0207.

Friendly little guesthouse right beside the main highway, five minutes' walk from the beaches, with a couple of rather dark but spacious self-catering apartments in winter/summer and two well-furnished rooms in the main house. ③/②

Escape

Map 5, C10. ✆ and fax 424 7571.

One of the best of the island's all-inclusive hotels – an unpretentious place warmly decked out in bright, pastel colours and popular with tour groups from Italy and England. Watersports are limited – no wave runners or skiing – but the beach is great and the food considerably better and more varied than at most of the similarly-priced all-inclusives. Ask for an ocean-view room on the second floor. Rates start at $275/$210 in winter/summer. ⑦

Smugglers' Cove

Map 5, C8. ✆432 1741, fax 432 1749.

Small, friendly but slightly cramped hotel, colourfully decked out with crotons, with 21 rooms – all with tiny kitchenettes.

There's a bar/restaurant and a small swimming pool, ten metres from the beach, and the place offers decent value on the expensive west coast, particularly during the summer. ⑤/④

Treasure Beach
Map 5, C9. ⍣432 1346, fax 432 1094.
Small, unpretentious and charming hotel, with large rooms, a small pool and some of the friendliest staff around. ⑦/⑥

AROUND HOLETOWN

Glitter Bay
Map 5, C5. ⍣422 4111, fax 422 1367.
Elegantly designed, furnished and landscaped, Mediterranean in style, with a large pool and good watersports. Top quality – the rooms are spectacular and the service impeccable. ⑦

Golden Palm
Map 5, C7. ⍣432 6666, fax 432 1335.
Three-storey apartment block right by the sea, rather functional in design but with seventy spacious suites, each with their own kitchens, living rooms, fans and a-c. There's a small pool, a restaurant and bar, a couple of decent beaches nearby and good snorkelling right offshore. ⑥/④

Inn On the Beach
Map 5, C7. ⍣432 0385, fax 432 2440.
Small hotel with large, comfortable air-conditioned rooms and oceanfront balconies overlooking a good beach, very close to Holetown's multiple shopping facilities. ⑥/④

Sandy Lane

Map 5, C7. ℂ432 1311, fax 432 2954.

The jewel of the west coast, a magnificent place in every way – but if you need to ask the price you can't afford it. ⑦

Settlers' Beach

Map 5, C6. ℂ432 0840, fax 432 2147

Delightful apartment hotel on a great stretch of beach, attractively landscaped; the large rooms make it a good choice for families. ⑦/⑤

Sunset Crest Resort

Map 5, C7. ℂ432 6750, fax 432 7229.

Large, sprawling resort ten minutes' walk from the beach, with several swimming pools, restaurants and bars, and over a hundred one-, two- and three-bedroom apartments scattered around the complex. Rates for the rather tatty smaller rooms start at $80/55 in winter/summer, though it's worth paying a few dollars extra for the more secluded Travellers' Palm apartments. Two-bedroom villas rent for $120/85, with a $10 per person surcharge if there are more than two of you. ④/③

AROUND SPEIGHTSTOWN

Almond Beach Village

Map 5, B1. ℂ422 4900, fax 422 0617.

Popular all-inclusive, by far the largest hotel on the island, spread along a lengthy stretch of beach just north of Speightstown, with a wide range of bars, restaurants and activities. ⑦

King's Beach Hotel
Map 5, B3. ✆422 1690, fax 422 1691.

Large, well-designed and attractive place, popular with German and Dutch package tourists, beautifully landscaped and with plenty of feeling of space. The beach is gorgeous and there's an extensive array of free watersports if you get past the pool.
⑦/⑤

Sandridge Hotel
Map 5, B3. ✆422 2361, fax 422 1965.

Three-storey hotel on a lovely strip of beach edged with tall coconut palms, and as good value as you'll find on the west coast. The rooms are sizeable, there are two restaurants and a large pool, and there's great snorkelling just offshore.
⑤/④

THE EAST COAST

A handful of small but characterful places on the surf-lashed and little-touristed **east coast** offer a change from the built-up south and west of the island. Unless you're really looking to get away from it all, you probably won't want to spend your entire trip here, but it's a great, quiet spot to unwind for a couple of days, walking on the deserted beaches and escaping the crowds.

Atlantis Hotel
Map 2, 5E. Bathsheba, ✆433 9445, no fax.

Ancient, faded and extremely welcoming place overlooking Tent Bay, with great food that brings people from all round the island and eight modest rooms; ask for one with a balcony.
③

THE EAST COAST

The Edgewater Inn

Map 2, D5. Bathsheba, ☎433 9900, fax 433 9902.

 An attractive place just above beautiful Bathsheba. Most of the
rooms are pretty ordinary, but a couple of them, 221 and 218,
have balconies and great sea views, and go for a higher rate
(negotiable when things are quiet). There's a pool and
hammocks, and the hotel offers guided hikes into the nearby
rainforest. ④

Kingsley Club

Map 2, D5. Cattlewash, ☎433 9422, fax 433 9558.

Slightly faded but very easygoing and engaging place, with
seven comfortable, wood-floored rooms facing out to the
crashing surf of the Atlantic past the palms and casuarina trees.
There's a permanent light breeze and, with an excellent
restaurant and bar, it's a great, quiet place to chill out for a
couple of days, walking on the deserted east coast beaches and
escaping the crowds. ⑤/④

Round House Inn

Map 2, D5. Bathsheba, ☎433 9678

A good option if you're up here for the surfing, this friendly,
newly refurbished place is more of a restaurant than a hotel, but
the owners rent out a couple of rooms upstairs. ③

EATING AND DRINKING

espite the limited size of the island, the huge and still-expanding tourist market has produced a staggering variety of **places to eat**. Although most of Barbados's restaurants have a vaguely international flavour to cater for the foreign visitors, there is plenty of great local produce on offer, and it's well worth going out of your way to sample traditional Barbadian cuisine.

At the cheapest end of the market, there are plenty of fast-food outlets across the island though, refreshingly, many of the big American chains have been kept at bay. Most popular of the local options is the *Chefette/Barbecue Barn* chain, distinctive by their enormous signs, where you can get reasonably priced pizzas, fried chicken, burgers and rotis (curried meat or vegetables wrapped in a flour pancake). Up a notch in price, the south coast in particular has a good sprinkling of places where you can get a meal for around B$12–15, though you'll find fewer of these on the generally more upmarket west coast, where prices for a main course tend to start around B$30 and, in chic places like the *Cliff*, not less than B$45–50.

Bajan food

As you'd expect, fresh **seafood** is the island's speciality: snapper, barracuda and dolphin fish (not the porpoise), as well as fresh prawns and lobster. Most popular of all, though, is the **flying fish** – virtually a Bajan national emblem. The fish doesn't really fly; accelerating up to 65kph it shoots out of the water and, extending its lateral fins like wings, glides through the air for up to thirty metres, usually to escape underwater pursuit, sometimes (it would seem) just for fun. Easy to fillet and prepare, flying fish make a cheap and tasty meal, and are found on restaurant menus across the country – there are even stores selling boxes of them on ice at the airport.

Most menus also feature **chicken** and **steaks**, and a lot of places include one or two relatively inexpensive pasta dishes. Look out, too, for traditional Bajan dishes: the national dish is **cou-cou** (a cornmeal and okra pudding) and saltfish, and you'll ocasionally find the fabulous **pudding and souse** – steamed sweet potato served with cuts of pork pickled in onion, lime and hot peppers. **Cohobblopot** (also known as pepperpot) is a spicy meat and okra stew. Dishes from the wider Caribbean, such as the fiery Jamaican-style jerk pork or chicken, are also popular.

`Vegetarians will have to work a bit to avoid meat or fish. There is a fantastic selection of **vegetables**, including the starchy **breadfruit** (best roasted) and the squash-like **christophene**, but many restaurants don't offer a single vegetarian option and you'll have to negotiate. Watch out too for the ubiquitous **peas and rice** (rice cooked with a variety of peas or beans) that accompanies many main dishes, as a piece of salted pork is usually chucked in to the pot for added flavour.

For **snacks**, you'll find **cutters** (bread rolls with a meat or cheese filling) and coconut bread in many bars and rum shops, while the more substantial **rotis** – flat, unleavened bread wrapped around a filling of curried meat or vegetables – are also widely available. Less frequently seen outside a Bajan home, but worth keeping an eye open for, are **conkies**, made from pumpkin, sweet potato, cornmeal and coconut, mixed and steamed in banana leaves.

Finally, don't miss out on the superb local **fruits**, from the mangos and paw paws that you may have seen abroad to the sapodillas and sweetsops that you almost certainly won't have encountered before.

As far as **drinking** is concerned, rum (see p.49) is the liquor of choice for many Bajans, from the basic white rums that form the basis for most cocktails to older, dark rums like Mount Gay's superb *Extra Old*. The local beer is *Banks* which, despite strong competition from the excellent *Red Stripe* of Jamaica and *Carib* of Trinidad, remains by far the most popular brew island-wide. Wine is an expensive option, though you'll occasionally find Californian whites and reds at reasonable prices.

Hundreds of tiny **rum bars** dot the island; they are an integral part of Bajan social life, and are great places to stop off for a drink and a chat if you're touring. On the coast, you'll find fewer places that cater specifically for drinkers but, all-inclusives apart, most hotels and restaurants will welcome you for a drink even if you're not staying or eating.

BRIDGETOWN

There's a reasonable selection of places to grab a snack while you're sightseeing in Bridgetown and, although few people make the trip into the city specifically to eat, there are also a couple of of excellent restaurants that open in the

Restaurant prices and reservations

In the reviews that follow, restaurants have been graded as inexpensive (under B$40 a head for a three-course meal without drinks), moderate (B$40–60), expensive (B$60–80) and very expensive (over B$80). During the winter season (Dec–April) it's worth making a reservation at many of the places recommended and, if you've got your heart set on a special place, arrange it a couple of days in advance if you can.

evening. If you're in town at night drinking or clubbing, you might want to check out the late-opening local joints on busy **Baxters Road**, just north of the town centre, where you can get a plate of food for around B$10.

The Boatyard
Map 3, F6. Bay Street (✆436 2622).
Daily 6–10pm. Moderate.
More a nightclub than a restaurant, but it does have a decent selection of moderately priced food, including grilled fish, burgers and pizza, to soak up the beer and the rum.

Brown Sugar
Map 2, B8. Aquatic Gap (✆427 2329).
Daily 6–9.30pm. Expensive.
Attractive little building with iron fretwork and an interior draped with greenery, serving the best seafood in the area and good pasta, with prices starting around B$25.

High Crust
Map 3, G2. 34 Roebuck St.
Mon–Fri 10am–5pm. Inexpensive.

This small snack bar just north of the central bank is a good place for patties, cakes and juices while you're exploring.

Jeff Mex
Map 3, D4. Broad St (☏431 0857).
Daily 10am–5pm. Inexpensive–moderate.
Burritos, enchiladas and fajitas on the Mexican side, all from around B$15, and similarly-priced burgers, subs and steaks for those after a North American option.

Nelson's Arms
Map 3, D4. Galleria Mall, 27 Broad St (☏431 0602).
Daily 11am–3pm. Inexpensive–moderate.
Large, popular pub in the heart of duty-free shopping land – nautically themed, and suitably decorated with sailors and pirates – that makes for a decent lunch break, with flying fish, chicken, pasta and rotis for B$15-25.

The Rusty Pelican
Map 3, E5. Careenage (☏436 7778).
Mon–Sat noon–2pm & 6–10pm, Sun 6–10pm. Moderate.
This new, moderately priced restaurant above the *Waterfront Café*, offers a huge menu of burgers, steaks, chicken, pasta and sandwiches and great views over the Careenage and the parliament buildings.

The Vegetarian
Map 2, B8. Stanmore, Black Rock (☏425 6258).
Daily 5–7pm. Inexpensive.
A little tricky to find, but worth the journey if you're after

BRIDGETOWN

good, authentic veggie food – bean stews, lentil roast and stir-fried granburger all for B$12, as well as vegetarian rotis, burgers and cakes and several fresh fruit juices to wash it all down.

The Waterfront Café
Map 3, E5. Careenage (✆427 0093).
Mon–Sat noon–3pm & 6–10pm, Sun 6–10pm. Moderate.
Some of the best food in town, with an authentic Caribbean flavour, served indoors or out beside the water. Try the creole snapper or grilled barracuda with cou-cou – both around B$35 – or, if you're just after a snack, you can get cutters, soups and salads. There's live music most evenings, normally steel pans (Tues & Wed) and jazz (Fri & Sat), and a huge buffet dinner (Tues).

THE SOUTH COAST

You'll find the widest variety of places to eat on the south coast, particularly at the crowded **St Lawrence Gap**, where street vendors flogging jerk chicken and hot dogs jostle with punters heading for the classy oceanfront restaurants. If you're staying on this side of the island, don't miss out on a meal at the *Bay Garden* in **Oistins**, where there's a good Bajan-tourist mix, and fish fresh from the boat.

HASTINGS

Champers
Map 4, B5 (✆435 6644).
Daily 6–10pm. Moderate–expensive.
Attractive wine bar-restaurant right on the oceanfront, serving decent steak and seafood main courses for B$20–45; there's also a wide variety of wines.

Jeff Mex
Map 4, B5. Chattel Plaza (☎435 6363).
Mon–Sat 11am–11pm, Sun 6–10pm. Inexpensive–moderate.
Regular Mexican food, including good chicken and steak
fajitas and vegetarian enchiladas, with prices from around
B$12.

39 Steps
Map 4, B5. Chattel Plaza (☎427 0715).
Mon–Fri noon–midnight, Sat 6pm–midnight. Moderate.
Fashionable, atmospheric and moderately priced wine bar; the
chalked-up daily specials normally include several excellent fish
dishes, as well as good soups and salads.

ROCKLEY

Bubba's Sports Bar
Map 4, C4 (☎435 6217).
Daily 10am–10pm. Inexpensive–moderate.
The food is very much secondary to the entertainment here,
with large and small TV screens dotted around the place
showing sport from around the world, but you can get decent
and reasonably priced burgers, chicken, steaks and sandwiches
to munch while you gawp.

Gilligan's
Map 4, C4. *Riviera Beach Hotel*.
Mon–Fri noon–2pm & 6–9pm. Inexpensive.
Nothing to write home about, but you can get a reasonable
meal of fish and chips or grilled chicken with rice and peas for
B$15.

ROCKLEY

Buddies

Map 4, E5. Opposite the *Sandy Beach* resort (©435 6545).
Daily 5.30–10.30pm. Inexpensive–moderate.
Friendly, easygoing place, serving freshly made soups, pasta
dishes for B$16-20 and great salads with blackened tuna or
dolphin fish for a little less. A lively spot for late-night drinkers,
especially at weekends.

Carib Beach Bar

Map 4, E5. Next to the *Crystal Waters* guesthouse.
Daily 11.30am–10pm. Inexpensive–moderate.
A lively place for a drink, especially during the early evening
happy hour from 5pm to 6pm, when you'll also get reasonaly
priced snacks.

Guang Dong

Map 4, E5. (©435 7387).
Daily 11am–2pm & 6–10pm. Moderate.
Solid Chinese restaurant, offering typical dishes of sweet and
sour, chow mein and chop suey, from B$15, with particularly
good lunchtime combo deals for B$16.

Roti Hut

Map 4, D5.
Mon–Sat 11am–10pm, closed Sun. Inexpensive.
Good place to munch on inexpensive rotis – options include
potato rotis for B$3.50, chicken and potato for B$8 and shrimp
for B$9.

Shells Guesthouse
Map 4, E5.

Daily 5.30–9pm. Moderate.

Small, brightly coloured and unpretentious restaurant with a
daily-changing blackboard menu; typical offerings include
flying fish or barbecued chicken with rice and peas for B$22 or
a full-blown three-course dinner for B$40.

ST LAWRENCE GAP

Bellini's
Map 4, F5. (✆435 7246).

Daily 6–10pm. Moderate–expensive.

Popular Italian place overlooking Little Bay, with basic pasta
dishes starting at B$30 and more interesting options from
B$45, including poached kingfish with shrimps in pesto sauce,
or grilled swordfish in dill and white wine.

Café Sol
Map 4, F5. (✆435 9531).

Daily 6–11pm. Moderate.

Lively, often crowded Mexican place doing a roaring trade in
margaritas and Mexican beers, particularly during the happy
hours 6–7pm and 10–11pm; the food sometimes feels
secondary, but you'll get decent and sensibly priced chicken,
beef and vegetarian burritos, tacos and enchiladas.

Captain's Carvery at the Ship Inn
Map 4, F5. (✆435 6961).

Mon–Fri 11.30am–2.30pm, daily 5.30–9.30pm. Moderate.

Huge, nautically themed pub, with a good range of beers and

food, and regular live music. All-you-can-eat buffet options for lunch and dinner (B$21 and B$40 respectively), specializing in roast meats – usually a selection of beef, pork and turkey – served with baked potatoes and a variety of salads.

Josef's

Map 4, F5. (©435 6541).
Daily 6–10pm, Dec–April also noon–2pm. Expensive.
Both the food and the service are as good as you'll find on the south coast at this elegant coral stone restaurant, with candelit tables indoors and down by the water's edge. Starters run B$8-22 and include soups, chargrilled shrimp and beef carpaccio; main courses of blackened dolphin, roast chicken or rack of lamb start at B$35.

McBride's Pub

Map 4, F5.
Daily 5pm–midnight.
The inevitable Irish pub – yes, they do serve *Guinness*. Usually crowded with twenty-something holidaymakers, and blaring out the latest in Britpop.

Pisces

Map 4, F5. (©435 6564).
Daily 5.30–10pm. Moderate–expensive.
Cavernous but attractive waterside restaurant with a strong emphasis on seafood – catch of the day, usually snapper or dolphin, costs around B$30 – though the service can be rather hit-and-miss.

ST LAWRENCE GAP

Roti Den

Map 4, F5. (✆435 9071).
Daily 5.30–9pm. Inexpensive.

Top-rate, inexpensive rotis – try the particularly good
vegetarian option with channa, pumpkin and potato – as well
as full meals of curried or fried chicken or fish with rice and
peas for around B$13.

St Lawrence Pizza Hut

Map 4, G5. (✆428 7153).
Mon–Sat 5.30–9pm. Inexpensive–moderate.

Not the most exciting place in the area, but a decent option for
filling up on inexpensive pizzas and pastas before you go
clubbing in the Gap (see p.168).

MAXWELL

Angie's Restaurant

**Map 4, H5. On the waterfront just east of the *Sea Breeze Hotel*
(✆428 5380).**
Daily 11.30am–2.30pm & 5.30–10pm. Moderate.

Lively spot with burgers and sandwiches for lunch from around
B$7 and good fish and chicken dishes at night from B$25. Every
Wednesday evening there's a rum punch party with live music.

Gideon's Inn

Map 4, H5.
Mon–Sat 5.30–9pm. Moderate.

Rustic local spot at the west end of the coast road, somewhat
hit-and-miss as far as service is concerned, but with good
seafood meals from B$25 – flying fish, shrimp and lobster
specialities.

MAXWELL

The Mermaid
Map 4, H5. (✆428 4116).
Daily 6–9.30pm. Moderate–expensive.

Rather more elegant than *Gideon's*, at the other end of the strip, with views over the water, and regular theme nights – barbecues on Tuesday, seafood on Friday and West Indian buffet on Sunday – with prices from B$40.

OISTINS AND SILVER SANDS

The Bay Garden
Map 4, K4. Oistins Market.
Daily 5.30–10pm. Inexpensive.

One of the most atmospheric places on the island, with a dozen stalls offering a variety of seafood from spicy conch fritters to huge plates of fried kingfish or dolphin, served with peas and rice and vegetables. Prices are low: you'll be hard-pressed to pay more than B$12 a head, and if you go into the covered *Fish Net* area you'll find plenty of Bajans tucking into equally good barbecued fish straight off the grill.

Cathy's Bar
Map 4, K4. Oistins Market.
Daily 5–11pm.

This typical Bajan rum shop in the centre of the Oistins Market is a good place to grab a drink and meet some of the locals before heading to the *Bay Garden* for your fish dinner.

Round Rock Apartment Hotel
Map 2, E9. Silver Sands (✆428 7500).

Daily 11am–2pm & 5.30–9.30pm. Moderate.
Similar food to the *Silver Rock*, served on an attractive veranda
overlooking the sea, and with a popular Caribbean buffet lunch
and dinner on Sunday.

Silver Rock Hotel

Map 2, E9. Silver Sands (⌀428 2866).
Daily 8am–9pm. Moderate.
Good food at the beachside restaurant, with a full cooked
"surfer's breakfast" for B$10, lunchtime sandwiches and
burgers for B$7-10 and evening meals of fish, steaks and lobster
from around B$25.

THE SOUTHEAST

Castle View

Map 2, G7. Outside the entrance to *Sam Lord's Castle*
(⌀423 5674).
Daily 6–9.30pm. Moderate.
This delightful little place serves great cocktails, and the meals
are good value, with flying fish, steak or chicken with fries or
rice and peas for B$16-24.

Crane Beach Hotel

Map 2, G8. (⌀423 6220).
Daily 11.30am–2pm & 5.30–9.30pm. Expensive.
Normally the best food in the southeast, with a restaurant
that overlooks the bay and serves excellent and innovative
seafood dishes, and a good lunch stop if you're making a day
trip to the area. Bear in mind, though, that prices are on the
high side, and that the place tends to lack atmosphere out of
season.

THE SOUTHEAST

THE WEST COAST

Plenty of top-notch restaurants line the "platinum coast", serving the well-heeled residents of the area's many plush homes and hotels. Several of them as good as anything you'll find anywhere in the Caribbean. You'd have to look a little harder to find interesting low-priced options, but they do exist, and several of them – including the *Fishermen's Pub* in Speightstown and the *Garden Bar* at *Angler's Apartments* are definitely worth checking out, whatever your budget.

PROSPECT TO PAYNES BAY

Bombas

Map 5, C9. Prospect (℡432 0569).
Daily 11am–11pm. Moderate–expensive.
Casual beach bar offering inexpensive roti, chicken and fish snacks during the day and changing daily pasta, curry and vegetarian specials for B$30–40 in the evening.

Bourbon Street

Map 5, C10. Prospect (℡424 4557).
Daily 6pm–midnight. Expensive–very expensive.
New Orleans comes to Barbados at this top-notch Cajun restaurant, serving crawfish, oysters, jambalaya and etouffe to the strains of Preservation Hall jazz, on an atmospheric covered terrace just above the sea. Much of the fresh produce is flown in direct from Louisiana, so prices are fairly hefty – around B$20 for most starters, B$50-60 for main dishes. The bar stays open until 1am, and they'll often set up some dancing space after the diners have finished.

Carambola
Map 5, C10. Prospect (✆432 0832).
Mon–Sat 6.30–10.30pm. Expensive–very expensive.
Excellent Caribbean food in a lovely outdoor setting on cliffs
overlooking the ocean. Soups start at B$12, other starters –
smoked duck salad, scallops with coconut and lemon grass – cost
around B$25, while main courses include blackened dolphin for
B$48, seared tuna in a tomato and caper sauce for B$53 or pasta
with red peppers, pine nuts and artichokes for B$40.

The Cliff
Map 5, C9. Fitts (✆432 1922).
Daily 6–10.30pm. Expensive–very expensive.
If you're only going to splash out once on a great dinner while
you're in Barbados, you could hardly pick a better place than
The Cliff – a beautiful, pillared coral stone restaurant on
another cliff-top location, with a small army of waiters, flaming
torches and the most exquisite food. Expect to pay B$75-90
for two courses before drinks.

Coach House
Map 5, C8. Paynes Bay (✆432 1163).
Daily 5.30–midnight.
This lively place recreates the style of a traditional English pub,
with indoor and outdoor bars. It's often a good place to catch
live bands (see p.170).

Crocodile's Den
Map 5, C9. Paynes Bay (✆432 7625).
Daily from 5pm.
Funky cocktail bar, with pool, darts and board games, canned

and (occasional) live music, satellite sports and a great late-night atmosphere.

Fathoms
Map 5, C9. Paynes Bay (℗432 2568).
Daily noon–3pm & 6.30–10pm. Expensive.
Reasonable value, well-presented food, served on a terrace overlooking the sea. Seafood is the speciality, with starters at B$19 including octopus ceviche and shrimp and crab etouffe, and main dishes including barracuda, kingfish and snapper, all for B$42. Slightly cheaper, there are also a couple of pasta options and chicken or shrimp salads for around B$30.

Garden Bar
Map 5, C9. Angler's Apartments (℗432 0817).
Daily 6–8.30pm. Inexpensive.
Small, laid-back, no-frills place offering traditional West Indian meals like pepperpot, cook-up rice (rice and peas with salt beef and lamb, cooked in coconut milk) and, occasionally, Guyanese specialities like metagee – a root vegetable stew of plantains, cassava, eddoes and dumplings served with shredded beef or fish. Reckon on around $25 a head.

Islands
Map 5, C8. Sunset Crest (℗432 1163).
Daily 5.30–10pm. Moderate–expensive.
Fun, colourful and moderately priced Caribbean restaurant with a penchant for cooking dishes at your table – "garlic prawn whoosh", flamed in Malibu, and crêpes suzettes among the most extravagant – with a host of more traditionally prepared options like pepperpot soup, jerk pork and local snapper and dolphin fish.

Marshalls
Map 5, D9. Holders Hill.
Daily noon–2pm & 5–9pm. Inexpensive.
Easygoing local bar serving a wide selection of single dishes for
around B$15 – try the curried chicken, flying fish or stewed
beef, all served with rice and peas, macaroni pie and salad.
Head uphill, past Holders Great House, and the restaurant is on
your left, opposite the playing field.

Rose and Crown
Map 5, C10. Prospect (☎425 1074).
Daily 11am–2pm & 6–10pm. Moderate.
Decent, long-standing local seafood restaurant offering the
catch of the day from B$28, seafood kebabs for B$35, and a
variety of lobster dishes for B$60.

HOLETOWN

Angry Annies
Map 5, C7. 1st Street (☎432 2119).
Mon–Sat 6–10pm. Expensive–very expensive.
Brightly painted building just off the main highway, with a
decent selection of local food – starters of fisherman's soup or
flying fish fillets for around B$13, main courses of lamb in
mustard sauce or garlic lobster for B$70.

Kitchen Korner
Map 5, C6.
Daily 11.30am–2.30pm. Moderate.
Run in association with the excellent *Olive's* (see below), this
little café is a good spot for lunch if you're in town, offering
simple, tasty cooking and the likes of panfried flying fish,
curried chicken roti or fusilli with pesto sauce for B$15-25.

HOLETOWN

The Mews

Map 5, C7. (✆432 1122).
Daily 5.30–11pm. Expensive–very expensive.
Austrian chef Josef Schweigler has blazed a trail in New Caribbean cuisine since arriving in Barbados in 1982; his latest restaurant continues the trend with unforgettable food in this initially unpromising Holetown townhouse – ask for a table on one of the upstairs terraces. The seafood is imaginative and magnificent, and the place is usually packed with local bigwigs. Reckon on B$15-25 for starters, B$45-65 for main courses, and don't miss the baked white chocolate cheesecake.

Olive's Bar & Bistro

Map 5, C6. (✆432 2112).
Daily 6–10pm. Moderate–expensive.
Popular Holetown eatery, simple in design with its wooden floor and white tablecloths, but offering a wide choice of excellent meals. Regular starters include beef carpaccio or warm shrimp salad for B$19-B$22, with main courses of fettucini with tomato and basil sauce (B$26), jerk pork with roasted garlic mash (B$40) or seared sea scallops with rice and curry sauce (B$56).

Peppers

Map 5, C6. (✆432 7549).
Mon–Sat 11.30am–10pm. Expensive.
Pleasant little place just off the highway, full of greenery and with an easygoing, mellow atmosphere. Food is standard West Indian with a couple of excellent specialities, like Dominican crab backs and jerked marlin, and you'll pay B$30-40 for most of the entrees. On Friday night, when a Latin band plays, they clear away tables for the dancers, and there's a more mellow jazz/blues night on Saturday.

HOLETOWN

Tam's Wok
Map 5, C6. 1st Street (℠432 8000).
Daily 11am–2.30pm & 6–10pm. Moderate.
Best Chinese food in the area, with a lively host and a familiar
menu that includes excellent sweet and sour dishes from B$26,
chow meins for B$20 and plenty of good vegetarian and
seafood options.

MULLINS BAY TO SPEIGHTSTOWN

Chattel House
Map 5, B3. Sandridge Beach Hotel.
Daily 11am–9pm. Inxpensive–moderate.
Slightly sanitized but hugely engaging version of a typical Bajan
rum shop, brightly painted with traditional wooden furniture and
enthusiastic service and serving good inexpensive cutters, burgers,
pies and chicken. If you're around on a Saturday, don't miss the
weekend special of pudding and souse – an absolute steal at B$8.

Fisherman's Pub
Map 5, B2. Queen Street (℠422 2703).
Daily 11am–10pm. Moderate.
Delightful place, with a large veranda jutting out over the
ocean, and the best value food in town. You can munch on a
sizeable roti or flying fish cutters at lunch-time for around B$5;
at night, typical Bajan dinners cost around B$20.

Mango's
Map 5, B2. Speightstown (℠422 0704).
Mon–Fri 6–10pm. Expensive.
Classy, popular restaurant offering friendly service and

MULLINS BAY TO SPEIGHTSTOWN |

top-notch local cooking from an extensive menu. Starters B$8–24, main courses B$25–55.

Mullins Beach Bar
Map 5, B5. (℗422 1878).
Daily 8.30am–10.30pm. Moderate.
Great location on Mullins Beach, and one of the busiest bars on the west coast, with tables spread over a wide ocean-view veranda offering reasonably priced all-day dining.

THE EAST COAST

You can't go wrong for lunch or dinner at any of the three **east coast** hotels, which all offer good home-style cooking with an emphasis on traditional Bajan food, while the *Round House Inn* is a welcome newcomer that offers a bit more in the way of innovation.

Atlantis Hotel
Map 2, D5. Bathsheba (℗433 9445).
Daily noon–2pm & 6–9pm. Moderate.
Faded old hotel with loads of character and great home cooking; the huge spreads at the lunchtime buffet are particularly good value at B$25. The large number of locals who keep coming back is as good a recommendation as you'll get.

The Edgewater Inn
Map 2, D5. Bathsheba (℗433 9900).
Daily noon–3pm & 6–10pm; buffet Mon–Sat noon–2pm. Moderate.
Whopping buffet lunches on offer at this charming old hotel

B$30 with chicken, fish, rice and peas, various salads and desserts, and a grander 'Bajan feast' for B$40 on Sunday lunchtimes that includes traditional foods like cou cou, pudding and souse and pickled breadfruit. The evening à la carte menu features some interesting options, as well as the Barbadian standards – grilled jerk chicken salad for B$20 or crispy coconut flying fish for B$25.

Kingsley Club
Map 2, D5. Cattlewash (☎433 9422).
Daily noon–2pm & 5.30–9.30pm. Moderate.
This large, friendly and very easygoing place serves good cutters, fish and salads. It's quite a wait for the food, but invariably worth it.

Round House Inn
Map 2, D5. Bathsheba (☎433 9678).
Daily 11.30am–2.30pm & 6–10pm. Moderate–expensive.
Top quality cooking and a casual, family atmosphere, halfway down the steep hill that plunges down to Bathsheba bay. The lunch and dinner menus are similar – offering dishes like blackened snapper, pan-fried flying fish or grilled jumbo shrimp for around B$35 – but you can also get sandwiches and salads at lunchtime for B$14 and up. There's an ocean view and you can sit indoors or on the veranda.

THE EAST COAST

ENTERTAINMENT AND NIGHTLIFE

I f you want to see Bajan **entertainment** at its very best, you'll need to visit during one of the major festivals, particularly the summertime **Crop Over** or April's **Congaline Carnival** (see p.171). At other times, the entertainment scene is rather more modest, with around a dozen decent nightclubs scattered around the island offering live and canned music, particularly in St Lawrence Gap on the south coast and in the capital Bridgetown.

Away from the clubs, several boats offer day and night "**party cruises**" (see p.175) and a handful of venues lay on tourist-oriented "dinner shows" where your entrance fee gets you supper and a live performance, usually of traditional music and dance. The best places to find out what's on during your stay are the free magazines *Sunseeker* and *The Visitor* given out by the tourist board and available at many of the hotels.

MUSIC

Calypso is the dominant music of Barbados and its modern descendant soca (soul calypso) holds sway in the island's nightclubs – lively, up-tempo music guaranteed to get you into dancing mode. You can catch a band playing most nights of the week at one of the clubs in St Lawrence Gap, and a couple of excellent beachside venues on the eastern edge of Bridgetown (just west of Hastings) also have live bands at the weekends. Many of these places double up as regular nightclubs for the rest of the week, often featuring "free drinks" nights on the quieter evenings, when a cover of around B$20 gets you entry and all you can drink.

BRIDGETOWN

Bridgetown has some of the best venues on the island for nightlife – several of them with stages rigged up right on the beach – and it's worth going out of your way to try at least one of them.

1627 and All That
(✆428 1627).
Twice-weekly, 7.30–10pm.
Normally held in the atmospheric central courtyard of the Barbados Museum, *1627 and All That* is a slick show that relates, through storytelling and traditional music and dance, the history of the island since the British first landed here.

The Boatyard
Bay Street (✆436 2622).
8.30pm–1am.
Live bands play by the beach on Fridays and Sundays, and, with the DJs spinning records on Tuesdays and Saturdays, a B$20 cover gets you in and all you can drink.

BRIDGETOWN

Bajan music

For centuries, the folk music of Barbados has preserved musical traditions – particularly traditional **African drumming** – imported by the slaves who came to work the island's sugar plantations. The plantation owners tried to kill off this musical heritage, banning and burning drums and other instruments, but the music remained underground, surfacing only after the freeing of the slaves in 1834. Its most distinctive form was the "tuk" band, so named for the rhythmic beating sound of their main instrument, the big log drum, with a banjo or tin flute providing the melody. On public holidays, tuk bands toured their simple but lively songs from village to village, normally accompanied by a dancing cast of characters that included a stiltman and a shaggy bear.

By the early twentieth century, the influence of Trinidadian **calypso** music had reached Barbados, and calypsonians took on the tuk band's role as wandering minstels, spreading their songs of political satire and social comment around the island. However, the music remained frowned upon by the authorities and by those who wanted to "get ahead". Ironically, it took a white band – **the Merrymen** – to really popularize calypso in the 1960s, with traditional songs like "Sly Mongoose" and "Brudda Neddy". Their success helped to spawn a new group of performers that emerged in the years after independence in 1966, including the grandly named **Mighty Viper**, **Lord Summers** and **Mighty Gabby** (see below).

The 1970s saw the explosion of reggae from the ghettoes of Jamaica and, though the music never took off in the same way in comparatively well-off Barbados, its success in the dancehalls did trigger two new musical forms. The first was **spouge**, a sort of reggae/calypso hybrid that was briefly popularised by singer **Jackie Opel** in the early 1970s; the second, rather more enduring, was soul calypso or **soca**, which offered a more lively, danceable version of traditional calypso.

Today, the best-known performers in Barbados are its calypsonians, particularly Antony Carter, better known as the Mighty Gabby. Gabby's radical calypsos often provide a focus for issues of national concern: in "Jack", for example, he attacked a government minister who floated the idea of hotels having private beaches (Bajans are extremely proud of the fact that all of their beaches remain open to the public); in "Take Down Nelson", he demanded that the Bridgetown statue of British Admiral Nelson should be replaced with a Bajan figure.

Admittedly today, much of the live music you'll find around Barbados lacks some of the cutting edge of singers like Gabby and his equally brilliant contemporaries like **Grynner** and **Red Plastic Bag**, but given its tiny size you'll still find the island's musical life in surprisingly bullish form.

Harbour Lights

(*C*436 7225).

8.30pm–1am.

Open every night for a B$20 cover, with live music on Fridays and Saturdays, and all-you-can-drink beach parties on Mondays and Thursdays.

Le Mirage

Bridge House, Cavans Lane (*C*428 8115).

9pm–late.

The main club in town, absolutely packed at the weekend but with a different scene nightly, featuring reggae "oldies", European disco, the latest Jamaican dancehall and the occasional live band. Admission costs around B$10, the crowd is almost entirely Bajan, and nothing much happens until well after midnight.

BRIDGETOWN

Waterfront Café
The Careenage (✆427 0093).
6.30–10pm.

Live, mellow jazz by the water several nights a week, usually Monday and Thursday to Saturday, and always free, but call ahead to check. Bajan star sax player Arturo Tappin used to be a regular – he's since moved on to greater things but still drops in for the occasional session and, if you're very lucky, you may just catch him.

THE SOUTH COAST

St Lawrence Gap is the heart of south coast nightlife, with plenty of good options whether you want to see a band or just dance.

After Dark
St Lawrence Gap (✆435 6547).
10pm–3am.

The late night zone – a huge but cleverly laid out and atmospheric place with a dark, smoochy disco and a massive stage and dancefloor out the back for the live bands who play a couple of times a week. The bar – nearly 30m long – claims to stock every liquor you can name, and the crowd is a good mixture of Bajans and tourists, all dressed up to the nines and partying until 3am.

B4 Blues
7.30–10.30pm.
St Lawrence Gap (✆435 6560).

Gentle live entertainment most nights at this bar/restaurant with acoustic guitar, mellow blues and the occasional magician doing card tricks at your table.

Reggae Lounge
St Lawrence Gap (✆435 6462).
9pm–late.

Intimate, unpretentious club with a small bar up top and concrete steps down to the open-air dancefloor under the palm trees. The DJs love to play the latest Jamaican dancehall, but you'll also get "oldies" nights – Bob Marley, Jimmy Cliff, Peter Tosh – and live bands several times a week, usually Thursdays and Sundays.

Sandy Bank
Hastings (✆435 1234).
8pm–midnight.

Nightly entertainment on the open-air veranda, with live bands, steel pan music, karaoke, limbo dancers and comedy stand-ups.

Ship Inn
St Lawrence Gap (✆435 6961).
9pm–1am.

English pub in style, with several bars and a small, sweaty dancefloor, with the most tourist-friendly bands – reggae meets rap meets Marvin Gaye. There's music every night from around 10.30pm–12.30am and bands, and a big crowd, on Tuesdays and Saturdays.

THE WEST COAST

Nightlife on the "platinum coast" is generally pretty quiet, mostly limited to steel bands and floor shows laid on by the more exclusive hotels for their guests. Though there's not a great deal in the way of local entertainment options, there

THE WEST COAST |

are a couple of places where you'll occasionally find a Barbadian band.

The Coach House
Paynes Bay (✆432 1163).
8pm–2am.
Live music most nights, with the island's top soca and steel bands as well as more mellow acoustic stuff on Fridays and the occasional karaoke evening thrown in for good measure.

Crocodile's Den
Paynes Bay (✆432 7625).
8pm–3am; happy hour 9–10pm.
Late-opening bar with pool tables and darts that usually features live music on Fridays and Saturdays, with local bands, DJs and occasional Latin nights, where you'll be obliged to learn to dance the salsa along with everyone else.

Fisherman's Pub
Speightstown (✆422 2703).
6–11pm.
Usually the liveliest place in town, with a steel band on Wednesday nights, and occasional floor shows on the ocean-front veranda.

Peppers
Holetown (✆432 7549).
8–11pm.
Friday night is the big night for entertainment, with a lively Latin band and plenty of dancing; Saturday sees more mellow live jazz on the garden terrace.

THE WEST COAST

Crop Over and Carnival

The **Crop Over** festival, held every summer, traditionally celebrated the completion of the sugar harvest and the end of months of exhausting work for the field-labourers on the sugar estates. As with many countries' carnival, which immediately precedes a period of fasting, Crop Over carried a frenzied sense of "enjoy-yourself-while-you-may", as workers knew that earnings would now be minimal until the next crop. Alongside the flags, dances and rum-drinking, the symbol of the festival was "Mr Harding" – a scarecrow-like figure stuffed with the dried leaves of the sugarcane – who was paraded around and introduced to the manager of the sugar plantation.

Though Crop Over has lost some of its significance since the 1960s, with sugar replaced by tourism as the country's main industry, it's still the island's main festival and an excuse for an extended party. Things start slowly in early July, with craft exhibitions and band rehearsals, heating up in late July and early August with street parades, concerts and competitions between the tuk bands, steel bands and – most importantly – the battle for the title of calypso monarch, dominated in recent decades by the Mighty Gabby (see p.167) and Red Plastic Bag who, between them, have won nine times in the last thirty years.

The **Congaline Carnival** is held during the last week in April, with a varied package of mostly local music that includes soca, reggae, steelpan and calypso. Daily shows are held from mid-afternoon to late-evening, usually at Dover pasture near St Lawrence Gap, and other events around the island conclude with a May Day parade through Bridgetown from the Garrison Savannah to the Spring Garden Highway.

THE WEST COAST

171

Round House Inn
Bathsheba (℗433 9678).
6.30–11pm
Attractive and welcoming bar/restaurant and pretty much the only place to find regular live music in the area, with a decent jazz or reggae band on Tuesday and Saturday nights.

SPORT

The confirmed beach addict and the watersports fanatic are equally at home in Barbados, with a variety of great beaches to choose from and plenty of operators offering excellent **diving**, **snorkelling**, **water-skiing** and similar activities. **Windsurfing** and **surfing** are also world-class, particularly on the southeast and east coasts respectively.

Also on the water, a number of companies offer **boat or catamaran tours** along the coast; there's a **submarine** that cruises the coral reefs to watch the fish close-up; and you can charter boats for **deep-sea fishing**.

There are plenty of land-based sports facilities, too, including a couple of good **golf courses**, **horse-riding** stables and occasional hiking and mountain-biking trips.

DIVING AND SNORKELLING

Diving is excellent on the coral reefs around Barbados, with the good sites all off the calm west and southwest coasts, from Maycocks Bay in the north right round to Castle Bank near St Lawrence Gap. The island has plenty of reputable dive operators (see p.174), most of whom will lay

Watersports operators

Coral Isle Divers, Cavans Lane, Bridgetown (✆431 9068).
Dive Barbados, Aquatic Gap, Bridgetown (✆426 9947).
Exploresub Barbados, St Lawrence Gap (✆435 6542).
Hightide Watersports, *Sandy Lane Hotel*, St James (✆432 0931).
Maldivers, Fitts Village, St James (✆432 8211).
Scuba Barbados, St Lawrence Gap (✆435 6565).
West Side Scuba Centre, Holetown (✆432 2558).

on transport to and from your hotel. Prices can vary dramatically between diveshops – always call around for the best deal – but reckon on around US$45–50 for a single tank dive, US$70–90 for a two tank dive and US$60–70 for a night dive, including use of equipment.

Beginners can get a feel for diving by taking a half-day **resort course**, involving basic theory, a shallow water (or pool) demonstration and a single dive. The course costs around US$70-80, and allows you to continue to dive with the people who taught you, though not with any other operator. Full **open water certification** – involving theory, tests, training dives and four full dives – takes three to four days and is rather more variable in price – expect to pay US$350–450, depending on the time of year and how busy the operator is. Serious divers should consider a **package deal**; these may simply cover three or five two-tank dives (roughly US$210 and US$350 respectively), or may also include accommodation and diving. Prices for these can be pretty good value, with savings of up to twenty percent, particularly outside the winter season, and it's worth contacting the dive operators direct to find out their latest offers.

Snorkelling is excellent, too, again especially off the west coast, where there are plenty of good coralheads just off-shore. Several of the dive operators also take snorkellers on their dive trips – reckon on around US$10–15 for an outing, including equipment, though if you're with a friend who's diving you may be able to blag yourself a free trip. Many top hotels provide guests with free snorkelling gear, but if you're not at one of these, finding the equipment can be expensive – try the places listed in the box – and you may want to bring a mask and snorkel with you.

Snorkelling in safety

Every year there are a handful of accidents in Barbados when snorkellers get hit by speedboats or jet-skis. Unless you're snorkelling in a roped-off section, keep a look-out for other people using the area for watersports, and remember that you're not particularly easy to spot.

BOATS, CATAMARANS AND A SUBMARINE

There is no shortage of boat trips to be made around Barbados, with the emphasis – not, it must be said, everyone's cup of tea – normally on being part of a big crowd all having a fun time together. Most of the **cruise boats** charge a single price, including a meal and all the drinks you want and, as the alcohol kicks in, people get into dancing mode with the live or canned music. The **catamarans** offer similar trips, though usually with a smaller number of people on board and less in the way of entertainment. The *Atlantis Submarine* offers a taste of underwater adventure without getting wet. All these boats sail out of Bridgetown's

Shallow Harbour, but will pick up guests from any of the major resorts.

Atlantis Submarine

℡436 8929.

B$142 per person.

A rare opportunity to ride in a submarine and a great option to see under the sea for anyone who doesn't dive. A boat takes you out of the Bridgetown harbour to board the sub, which then submerges to 30–45m, cruising slowly above the seabed for around thirty minutes before it rises to rejoin the "mother ship". Everyone has a seat by a porthole, and spectacular views of the fish and the coral, backed by a commentary on what you're seeing from the co-pilot.

Bajan Queen

℡436 6424.

Wed 6–10pm & Sat 5–9pm; B$79 or B$89 with hotel pick-up.

Attractive sea-cruiser, designed in the style of a Mississippi riverboat, offering twice-weekly sunset cruises along the west coast. Trips include a buffet dinner, all your drinks and live music.

Harbour Master

℡430 0900.

Tues & Thurs 11am–4pm; B$95.

Massive four-decker boat that runs regular day tours, taking you up the coast to a beach for chilling out or snorkelling, with a buffet lunch and free drinks. It also runs evening trips (Tues & Thurs 6–10pm; B$123), with a floor show, a live band, dinner and drinks all included in the price, and a cheaper option (Sun 5–9pm; B$35), where you pay for your food and drinks and a DJ provides the entertainment.

Jolly Roger
©436 6424.
Tues, Thurs & Sat 10am–2pm; B$123.
Sleek, two-sailed "pirate ship" running west coast lunch
cruises, with the emphasis on drinking and dancing up on the
top deck, walking the plank and swinging from the yard-arm
into the sea.

Mona Lisa
©435 6565.
Short, two-hour cruises on a ten-metre catamaran, with
snorkelling stops on the reef or around one of the shipwrecks.

Tiami
©427 7245.
Three catamarans take west coast lunch cruises, the five-hour
trip including several beach/snorkelling stops, charging B$123
per person.

FISHING

Fishing is a way of life in Barbados, both as an industry and
as a sport, and if you are at all interested, the island is an
incomparable place to try your hand. Various charter boats
offer **deep-sea fishing** trips where you can go after
wahoo, tuna, barracuda and, if you're lucky, marlin and
other sailfish. Prices for a group of up to six people start at
around B$500 for a half-day, B$1000 for a whole day,
including rods, bait, food, drink and transport from your
hotel. If you are not part of a group, operators will fit you
in with another party if they can, and charge around

B$180 for a half-day. Regular **operators** include Billfisher II (✆431 0741), Cannon Charters (✆424 6107) and Blue Marlin Charters (✆436 4322), but if you hunt around at dockside, particularly in Bridgetown, you can find plenty of others.

If you want to experience Bajan fishing in the raw, go out with some local fishermen. Many will be grateful for an extra pair of hands – ask around at the main fishing settlements like Oistins (see p.65), Six Men's Bay (see p.111), or Tent Bay on the east coast (see p.121). You'll need to clarify in advance exactly what's expected of you; although it can be an exhilarating experience, pulling lobster pots and fishing nets is extremely tough work, and you may be at it for hours.

WINDSURFING AND SURFING

Barbados hosts regular **windsurfing** tournaments around Silver Sands on the southeast coast, which is reckoned to be as good for windsurfers as anywhere in the Caribbean. Several of the hotels in the area cater mainly or exclusively for windsurfers; boards can be rented beside the *Silver Rock Hotel* (✆428 2866) or at the *Silver Sands Hotel* (✆428 6001), and cost around US$20 per hour, $35 for half a day, or from the windsurfing schools (see p.65), whose prices for coaching border on the extortionate. Elsewhere on the island, there are no rental outlets but many of the hotels have their own windsurfers which you can use – if you're staying there – for no extra cost. **Surfing** is also excellent, particularly on the east coast at the Bathsheba "soupbowl" (see p.122). Boards can be rented from the *Round House Inn* in Bathsheba, and you can buy them at some branches of the Cave Shepherd department store.

OTHER WATERSPORTS

If you're after **waterskiing**, **jet-ski** rides or a speedy tow on an inflatable banana, most hotels can find a reputable operator for you – expect to pay around B\$45 for fifteen minutes of waterskiing and half that for banana rides or jet-ski rental. Hightide Watersports (©432 0931), in Sandy Lane Bay, is one of the most trustworthy operators. You'll also find guys with speedboats on many of the west coast beaches, though less so on the south coast where the water is often a bit too choppy. Bear in mind that though these operators are often cheaper, many of them are unlicensed and uninsured, and don't go with anyone unless you feel comfortable with their operation.

Similarly, you'll find local guys offering trips on a **hobie-cat** (a mini-catamaran) on many of the beaches; they'll usually want to crew the boat themselves unless you can convince them you're an expert. **Kayaks** can be rented from Kayaker's Point (©428 6750), just east of *Ocean Spray Apartments* near Oistins, for US\$5 per hour, \$20 per day, and they'll deliver one to your hotel free of charge.

Finally, Skyrider Parasail (©420 6362) offer ten-minute **parasailing** trips – towed behind a boat on a parachute, then winched back aboard – for B\$90 per person, and will pick you up from any west coast beach

GOLF

The beautifully landscaped 6000m course at *Sandy Lane* (©432 4563) is the only eighteen-hole **golf** course open to the public in Barbados and, particularly in high season, it can be difficult to get a tee time. Green fees at the course are B\$150, club rental a further B\$60. The other major course, *Royal Westmoreland*, is only open to members and guests staying at certain of the more exclusive hotels. There is also a decent nine-hole course at the *Club Rockley* resort (✆435 7873) on the south coast, where green fees are B$63, with rental of clubs an additional B$28.

EQUESTRIAN SPORTS

Barbados has a lively equestrian tradition. There are races every other Saturday (except during April) at the Garrison Savannah **racecourse** (see p.53), and at Sandy Lane in March. There are several **polo fields**; the most prestigious of them, at Holders Hill (see p.79) holds matches on Wednesdays and Saturdays from September to March.

Not surprisingly, the island has several good stables offering **riding tours.** Some of the best are run by Highland Outdoor Tours (✆438 8069, fax 438 8070), who offer a delightful two-hour ride around their plantation for B$120 or an all-day trip down to an east coast beach for B$240, including breakfast, lunch and rum punch. Good trips are also offered by the Caribbean International Riding Centre (✆433 1453 or 420 1246), who offer three options: an hour's tour of the Scotland district (see p.118) for B$70; a ninety-minute ride down to the beach for B$100, and a two and a half hour trip to the beach and back for B$155. All prices include transfers to and from your hotel.

DIRECTORY

AIRLINES American Airlines (℃428 4170); BWIA (℃426 2111); British Airways (℃436 6413); LIAT (℃434 5428).

AIRPORT DEPARTURE TAX For international flights, the departure tax is presently B$25, payable at the airport when you leave, in local currency only.

AMBULANCE Call ℃115 in emergency. Alternatively, the government's ambulance service is on ℃426 1113; Lyndhurst's private ambulance is on ℃426 4170.

AMERICAN EXPRESS The Amex rep is Barbados International Travel Services, Horizon House, McGregor Street, Bridgetown (℃431 2423; Mon–Fri 8.30am–4pm, Sat 8.30am–noon); they'll also cash personal cheques guaranteed by your Amex card.

BANKS Bridgetown: Barclays, Broad Street and Lower Broad Street; Scotiabank, Broad Street; Barbados National Bank, Broad Street and Fairchild Street. **Hastings:** Caribbean Commercial Bank in Hastings Place; **Worthing**: Scotiabank beside the *Sandy Beach Hotel*; CIBC, just across the road in Worthing Plaza. **St Lawrence Gap:** Royal Bank of Canada by the *Ship Inn* at the west end of the coast road, and Barclays at the other end, near *Shakey's*. **Speightstown** has half a dozen banks, including Barclays and CIBC, both in Speightstown Mall.

BOOKSHOPS Bridgetown: The Cloister Bookshop (☏426 2662), on Hincks Street, has the island's best selection of books, while the big Cave Shepherd store (☏431 2121) on Broad Street also has a good choice. Tovannah Bookshop (☏429 2461) on St Michael's Row has plenty of secondhand books at knock-down prices.

CHILDREN Calm, clear seas, shelving beaches, no serious health risks and a welcoming attitude make Barbados an ideal destination for babies, toddlers and children. Most hotels welcome families and give substantial discounts for children – those under twelve often stay free in their parents' room – but it's worth checking in advance whether they put any restrictions on kids, especially if you're heading for an all-inclusive. You may also want to check on babysitting facilities.

CUSTOMS AND IMMIGRATION Entering Barbados, customs allow a duty-free quota of 1 litre of spirits, 250 grammes of tobacco and 50 cigars or 200 cigarettes. The import of weapons and farm produce is heavily restricted, and you'll risk severe penalties if you try to import drugs.

ELECTRIC CURRENT The island standard is 110 volts with two-pin sockets, though a few of the older hotels still use 220 volts. Take adaptors for essential items; some upmarket hotels and guesthouses have them, but you shouldn't count on it.

EMBASSIES Australian High Commission, Bishop's Court Hill, St Michael (☏435 2834), British High Commission, Lower

Collymore Rock Street, St Michael (*©*436 6694), Canadian High Commission, Bishop's Court Hill, St Michael (*©*429 3550), United States Embassy, Broad Street, Bridgetown (*©*436 4950).

EMERGENCIES Police *©*112, fire *©*113, ambulance *©*115.

HOSPITALS Queen Elizabeth's Hospital (*©*436 6450), on Martindale's Road, Bridgetown, is the island's main public hospital; Bayview Hospital on St Paul's Avenue is private.

LAUNDRY Bridgetown: Love's, Roebuck Street (*©*426 1235), Steve's, Bay Street (*©*427 9119). **Hastings**: laundromat (daily 8am–7pm). **Worthing**: Southshore laundromat (*©*435 7438), just across the road from the *Summer Home on Sea* guesthouse.

LIBRARY Bridgetown: the public library is on Coleridge Street; books can be borrowed on payment of a one-off refundable deposit of B\$20.

MEASUREMENTS Barbados is officially metric, but you'll often find directions and quantities given in miles and pounds.

PHARMACIES Bridgetown: Cheapside Pharmacy, Cheapside (Mon–Fri 7.30am–5.30pm, Sat 7.30am–1.30pm; *©*437 2004), Knight's, Lower Broad Street (daily 8am–1pm, *©*422 5191). **Holetown**: Knight's, Sunset Crest, (daily 8am–noon). **Oistins**: Knight's, Southern Plaza (Mon–Sat 8am–8pm; Sun 8am–1pm). **Rockley**: Lewis' Drug Mart opposite the *Accra Beach Hotel*, (Mon–Fri 9am–6pm, Sat 9am–1pm, Sun 9am–noon). **Speightstown**: Knight's (Mon–Sat 8am–8pm & Sun 8am–1pm).

PHOTOGRAPHY Barbados is made for pretty pictures. Film is expensive, so take plenty with you. Watch out for humidity; carry silica gel in your camera bag, keep film cool and develop it quickly. Over-exposure can also be a problem; watch out for glare from the sea and sand, and try to take picures early or late in the day. Before photographing people, ask their permission – some (especially schoolkids) like it, others don't. Film processing centres on the island include: Speedy's, Chattel House Village, **St Lawrence Gap**; True Colour, Quayside Centre, **Rockley** (opposite *Accra Beach Hotel*); Cave Shepherd, Broad Street, **Bridgetown**; and Photo Finish, Sunset Mall, Sunset Crest, near **Holetown**.

POLICE Emergency ✆112.

POST OFFICE (Mon 7.30am–noon & 1–3pm, Tues–Fri 8am–noon & 1–3.15pm). **Bridgetown**'s main post office is on Cheapside (✆436 4800); there are branches at the airport, in **Speightstown** (almost opposite Arlington), **Oistins**, **Worthing** and **Belleplaine**.

SUPERMARKETS Bridgetown: Julie's Supermart (Mon–Thurs 8am–9pm, Fri & Sat 8am–10pm) is on Bridge Street, just north of the Fairchild Street bus station. Palmetto Street market (Mon–Thurs 7am–5.30pm, Fri & Sat 7am–9.30pm) has great selections of fruit and vegetables. **Hastings**: there's a village supermarket (Mon–Sat 8am–6pm) off the highway opposite the pink *Ocean View Hotel*. **Worthing**: several supermarkets are clustered at the west end of town, including Big B at the bottom of Rendezvous Road, and marginally less well-stocked Plantation right by the highway. **Oistins**: there's a Super Centre (Mon–Sat 8am–8pm) beside the main road just west of Oistins, while the market is the best place to get fresh fish. **Speightstown**: Jordans' supermarket.

TAXIS The best option is to ask your hotel or guesthouse to recommend someone local; if they can't help, try one of the following. **Bridgetown**: Nelson's (©426 3337); Independence (©426 0090); **Hastings**: Caribbee (©427 0240); **Rockley**: Rockley Taxi (©435 8211); **St James**: Sunset Crest (©432 0367); **Island-wide**: Co-op (©428 6565 & 428 0953).

TIME Barbados is on Eastern Standard Time, five hours behind GMT.

TIPS AND TAXES Most hotels and restaurants automatically add a five percent service charge, so check your bill to ensure you're not paying twice. At restaurants that don't, it's not usually expected but (of course) always appreciated.

WEDDINGS Barbados is a very popular wedding destination. There's no residential qualification, so you can marry on the day you arrive and, unless one of you is divorced or widowed, you'll only need a valid passport or certified birth certificate and a marriage license – get your hotel or tour operator to organize the latter.

CONTEXTS

A brief history of Barbados

The earliest settlers in Barbados were **Amerindians**, who came to the island in dug-out canoes from the Guianas in South America. The Arawak-speaking **Tainos**, a peaceful race of skilled farmers and fishermen, first arrived around 350 AD. They were followed around 1250 AD by the more sophisticated and warlike **Caribs**, who killed (and sometimes ate) the Taino men and enslaved the women, forcing the survivors to move to islands further west in the Caribbean chain.

Columbus, the first European visitor to the West Indies, never stopped at Barbados, but in the early sixteenth century, Spanish **slave-traders** arrived to collect Amerindians to labour in the gold and silver mines of New Spain. With nowhere to hide on the flat, exposed island, the surviving Caribs fled to more mountainous islands like St Lucia and Dominica, and by the mid-sixteenth century Barbados was uninhabited.

The British in Barbados

In 1624, the **first English settlement** in the West Indies was established on St Kitts. A year later, a party of English sailors landed in Barbados, claiming the island for their king, and in February 1627 eighty colonists landed at present-day Holetown. King Charles I granted control of the island to the Earl of Carlisle, and in 1629, Carlisle appointed Henry Hawley as governor. Hawley issued land to the wealthier colonists, helping to create a small elite of planters. He also appointed a Council of men from this elite to advise him. A decade later, under pressure from those colonists who had no political influence, a separate "assembly" or parliament was set up.

The planters had come to Barbados to make money, and they experimented with a number of crops – notably tobacco, cotton and indigo – before settling on **sugar**. The industry brought almost instantaneous prosperity; by the 1650s, Barbados was reckoned to be the wealthiest place in the New World.

Servants and slaves

As Barbados developed, a workforce was needed for the sugar plantations. Political and religious refugees were already arriving on the island from England by the 1640s, as well as transported convicts, but the main source of workers was to be **indentured labourers** escaping poverty in England and Scotland. In return for their passage to Barbados, these men and women signed contracts to work on the plantations without wages for up to seven years. The island seemed to promise them an exciting new life, but the reality was closer to slavery. They were bought and sold like property, and those who complained were often treated even more harshly – public floggings were not unheard of.

As reports of these conditions filtered home, the supply of British servants began to dry up, and the Barbadian planters turned to a new source of labour. Between 1640 and 1700, around 135,000 West **African slaves** were brought to Barbados, and the island slowly began to take on its present-day ethnic composition. A 1661 Act dictated virtually every aspect of the slaves' existence: they could not leave the plantation without permission, could not own property, and could not play musical instruments. They were considered too simple to understand religious faith, so there was no provision for their Christianization, and a master was allowed to punish or even kill his slave as he saw fit.

Naturally, there was resistance. Runaways fled for the island's woods and gullies but, unlike in Jamaica, there were no mountainous areas in which they could hide, and they were easily hunted down. The first **organized rebellion** came as early as 1649, with more sophisticated island-wide plots unearthed in 1675 and 1692, when dozens of alleged rebels were executed. On the whole, though, the white militias remained in full control, with powers to search slave homes for weapons and to execute any slave they considered seditious.

The changing fortunes of sugar

By 1700, the wonder days of Barbados sugar had passed. Huge fortunes had been made, but increased competition from Jamaica and the Leeward Islands had reduced profits. Combined with soil exhaustion and a series of natural disasters, this squeezed many of the small planters out of business. Thousands left, and the number of whites on the island fell by around half between 1675 and 1710. When the American Revolutionary War (1776–1783) disrupted food supplies, many planters were obliged to turn sugar fields over to the cultivation of crops to feed their labour force; in 1777 the Assembly described Barbados as "decaying and impoverished". The end of the war brought some bounce back to the sugar industry, and Nelson's 1805 victory over the French stabilized European sugar markets, making him a hero with Barbados's white population.

Planters, yeomen and poor whites

The Barbados **planters** were, almost without exception, English, Anglican and white. As the colony developed, this small elite – many of them descended from the original settlers – continued to hold power. A couple of steps down the social ladder, the **yeomanry** – hundreds of families with relatively small landholdings – played an important part in local agriculture. Most aspired to enter the planter class through economic success or marriage, but the island's social pattern had fallen into place by the early eighteenth century, and such an upward step proved increasingly hard to take.

Way down the ladder were the **"poor whites"**, an assortment of peasants, labourers and unemployed vagrants. Some found positions on the plantations as overseers and artisans, but many more were forced to turn to subsistence farming on the undesirable land ignored by the planters, or even to poor-relief and begging.

Free slaves

For the slaves, freedom was, of course, the ultimate aspiration. From the earliest days, there were examples of slave-owners freeing their slaves, usually posthumously in their wills, but occasionally as a reward for outstanding actions. **Freed slaves** typically headed for the towns, setting up small businesses if they could find capital, or working as tradesmen and vendors. Although a handful made progress in business, on the whole the freed slaves were at the periphery of society, with few civic rights and shunned by the white population. The old and infirm were often reduced to begging.

More significant as a social class were the **free coloureds**, the name given to the offspring of (usually) white men and black women slaves. Barbadian whites, nervous about the prospect of these mixed race children claiming a stake in their society, quickly took steps to dampen their ambition. Any child born to a black mother was automatically deemed a slave, even if the father was a wealthy white planter. Even if the father freed his child on its reaching adulthood, the child's civic rights were strictly curtailed. An Act of 1721 restricted the right to vote to whites only (a law which remained in place until 1831), and also stated that free coloureds could not give evidence in courts against whites. This caused serious difficulties for coloureds in business, unable to testify on their own behalf against white debtors. Nonetheless, a number of free coloureds became merchants and even planters, and some established prominent dynasties.

Towards emancipation

In 1807 the British government abolished the slave trade, immediately curtailing the transfer of slaves from Africa to the Caribbean. Given their preference for island-born slaves, the Barbadian planters were less affected by this than most of their West Indian counterparts. Far more threatening was the movement for the abolition of slavery itself, gathering pace in Britain under the leadership of William Wilberforce. Barbadian slave-owners made some small improvements in the slaves' working conditions and legal status, but the slaves realized that these were little more than a reluctant sop to the abolitionists. Rumours spread, claiming that emancipation had been proclaimed in Britain but was being blocked on the island. Frustration grew, and in April 1816 Barbados faced its only serious slave uprising.

Bussa's Rebellion – named after its alleged leader, an African slave from a plantation in St Philip – began in the southeast with attacks on property and widespread burning of the sugar fields, and quickly spread to all of the island's southern and central parishes. Several major battles were fought between the slaves – who may have coordinated the uprising on an island-wide basis – and the white militias and British troops. Within three days, however, the rebellion was crushed; just a handful of whites were killed, but over a thousand slaves were either killed in battle or executed afterwards. The authorities also took the opportunity to execute some prominent free coloureds whom they saw as dangerous enthusiasts for emancipation.

Emancipation and after

By the early 1830s the reformers in London had won the argument for the **abolition of slavery**, though the planters put up a serious fight for it to be delivered on their own terms. Thus, the 1834 Act, while ending slavery, brought in an apprenticeship system under which all slaves over the age of six were obliged to work unpaid for their former owners for a further six years. In addition, Barbadian slave-owners received a massive £1.75 million from London in compensation for the loss of their slaves, who totalled some 83,000.

The planters were quick to take advantage of the new system. If the apprentices were now "free", went their argument, then they could take care of themselves. Food rations given to the apprentices were some of the poorest in the West Indies, work relations on the plantations deteriorated and, as children under six were now legally free, estate-owners made no provision for their upkeep, resulting in malnutrition, child abandonment and increased infant mortality.

It was soon obvious that the planters were making a mockery of the transition period to freedom proper, and the British persuaded the Assembly to bring forward **full emancipation** to August 1, 1838. The planters remained confident that the new situation would work to their advantage; no longer responsible for the upkeep of their workers, they would have a large pool of cheap, unorganized labour desperate for work.

Some former slaves headed to the towns, particularly Bridgetown, but most had little choice but to continue work on the sugar estates. The white planters still ran Barbados; they owned almost all of the farmland, and controlled the Assembly which made the island's laws. The major schools remained white-only, and the planters stood firmly against educating their former slaves. It was not until 1878 that the principle of **compulsory elementary education** was enshrined in law. Public welfare was minimal, resulting in the growth of large slums around Bridgetown and a spate of minor epidemics. Only when cholera hit the island – killing 20,000 people in 1853 – were steps taken to establish a nationwide **public health system**, and even then it remained poorly funded.

The rise of the merchants

By the 1880s the sugar industry was entering a crisis phase, largely induced by the drop in European sugar prices that followed the introduction of home-produced sugar beet. As debts mounted, more and more planters were forced to sell up to local merchants and financial institutions. For this **new business class**, the overriding social aspiration was to join the ranks of the planters. Apart from marriage, the purchase of a sugar estate was the only way into this social elite. On the whole, these merchants were white, and shared the values of the planters. The surviving members of the Barbadian plantocracy – now reinforced by the money and the backing of the merchant families – entered the twentieth century still in full control of the island's political and social infrastructure.

A Royal Commission and the Panama Canal

In 1897 the British government set up a **Royal Commission** to investigate the depressed West Indian sugar industry. Gradually, the planters accepted the recommended modernization, switching from the traditional small windmills to more efficient central processing factories.

Far more influential on the island's development was the decision by the United States in 1904 to build the **Panama Canal**. Tens of thousands of workers were needed, and by the outbreak of World War I Barbados had provided at least 20,000 – a huge percentage of the local workforce. Many returned with sizeable savings, which they were able to invest in new businesses and in land. The white planters, who had previously refused to sell land to blacks, were now obliged to do so by economic circumstances. Even if much of the land bought by blacks was marginal, by the 1930s the pattern of land ownership had changed dramatically.

Early black politics

During the 1920s, the influence of Jamaican Marcus Garvey and his black power movement also began to be felt in Barbados. In 1924, the island's first political party, the **Democratic League**, was founded by Charles Duncan O'Neale, a Garveyite who had spent time in England and Trinidad. The party's main support came from middle-class blacks and coloureds – very few of the working-classes had the right to vote – though it espoused a socialist programme and was popular with the poor. The party demanded compulsory education for blacks, the banning of child labour and an extension of the right to vote. However, the League was unable to make much headway against the vested interests of the island's white elite and, by the time of O'Neale's death in 1934, none of its major objectives had been achieved.

The 1937 rebellion

The worldwide depression of the 1930s hit Barbados hard. The price of sugar plunged, leading to unemployment and reduced wages amongst working-class blacks. A new radical leader, Trinidadian **Clement Payne**, arrived on the island in 1937, talking the language of exploitation of blacks by whites and encouraging workers to form **trade unions**. He also spread news of riots and strikes in other parts of the Caribbean. Alarmed by this fighting talk, the white authorities hastily arranged to have Payne deported. Within hours, **riots** broke out in Bridgetown and quickly spread to the countryside. It took three days for the rioting to be crushed, with fourteen blacks killed and over five hundred arrested.

Grantley Adams and political progress

Although many conservative blacks condemned the riots, it was obvious that a new outlet for working-class opinion was needed. In 1938, the **Barbados Progressive League** was founded – another black middle-class political party that aimed to improve conditions for those at the bottom of society. The leaders were divided about how best to accomplish this, with some arguing for step-by-step reforms and others seeking confrontation through the establishment of strong trade unions. Eventually, the more conciliatory wing of the party, led by future premier **Grantley Adams**, took control and assumed leadership of the organized black labour movement.

In 1939 the British government sent the **Moyne Commission** to Barbados to examine social and economic conditions. Adams worked closely with the commission to secure its support for improvements for the island's workers; in 1940, for example, trade unions were legalized. The 1943 **Representation of the People Act** increased the electorate fivefold (though it did not go as far as universal suffrage). As a result, the three parties that fought the 1944 election – Adams's Progressive League, the more radical black Congress Party and the Electors' Association of the white planters – shared the votes almost equally, with the black parties taking a total of fifteen seats to the planters' eight.

For the time being, though, executive power remained with the governor and the Executive Committee that he appointed. In 1946 Governor Bushe proposed that the political parties that won seats in an election should have the right to appoint members of the Committee and lent his preference to the Progressive League, now renamed the **Barbados Labour Party**. In 1950 Adams secured universal suffrage and in the 1951 election – playing to both black and white voters – his party took sixty percent of the popular vote. However, Adams' moderate political stance was antagonizing more and more members of his party and, although he retained power in the 1956 election, his party had already split, with the more radical members forming the **Democratic Labour Party** under the leadership of Erroll Barrow.

Federation

Adams was one of many Caribbean leaders after World War II who saw a federation of West Indian islands as the way forward for the region. With British support, it was decided that Trinidad should be the federal capital, and a federal government was elected in 1958. Adams himself stood successfully for election and was appointed federal prime minister, handing over the premiership of Barbados to Dr H.G. Cummins.

The experiment quickly ran into difficulties, however. Many people in Jamaica and Trinidad feared that they would have to support the small islands financially, while personal rivalry between regional leaders soured the atmosphere. The federal government that emerged was far weaker than many had hoped, with relatively small contributions from the island members and no power to raise taxes. Within three years Jamaica voted to leave the federation and was followed rapidly by Trinidad. In May 1962 the federation was officially dissolved.

Independence

In the elections of 1961 Erroll Barrow's Democratic Labour Party won office for the first time and the island saw some much-needed changes. To reduce the island's dependence on sugar, **foreign investment** was actively encouraged, and tourism, industrialization and other forms of agriculture such as livestock and vegetables were promoted. Free secondary education was provided from 1962, and the University of the West Indies established a campus on the island in 1963. Picketing was legalized and more adequate provision was made for injury compensation and severance pay for workers.

Although the sugar industry remained important, and the white planters and merchants retained powerful economic control in the island, the government's changes helped to create a new sense of purpose in Barbados. The British government finally recognized the capability of the Barbadians to govern themselves and, on November 30, 1966, after protracted negotiations, Barbados became an **independent country**.

INDEPENDENCE

A new country

Following the British tradition, Barbados developed a two-party political system. Barrow's Democratic Labour Party remained slightly left of centre, while the Barbados Labour Party tended to incorporate representatives of the planter and merchant class and so drifted to the right. Barrow remained prime minister until 1976 when the effects of the world economic crisis helped the Barbados Labour Party back to office.

Led now by **Tom Adams**, the son of former premier Grantley, the party soon faced accusations that it was acting as a puppet administration, both domestically on behalf of the island's white elite and internationally on behalf of the Americans. Adams was at the forefront of Caribbean support for the controversial American invasion of Grenada in 1983, and there was little challenge to the control of the white-owned companies that dominated Barbados's economic affairs.

Regionally, there has been talk of reviving a West Indian political federation, though no practical steps have yet been taken. Economically, however, the region has become far more integrated, establishing a free trade area in 1968 and expanding this, in 1973, into the **Caribbean Community and Common Market** (CARICOM), with double taxation treaties, a common external customs tariff and a unified system of incentives for industry. Barbados has been an important player in these developments and, with little of the political turbulence seen in places like Jamaica and Trinidad, economic progress has been rapid.

And, although the economic rewards have largely fallen to the large foreign- or white-owned banks and businesses, progress has stimulated the creation of a sizeable black professional middle-class, seen by some as the most distinctive social feature of the post-independence period. Gradually, too, Afro-Barbadian culture has pushed its way to the fore, with new music, dance and theatre groups, as well as local artists and writers expressing the social changes in Barbadian society.

Today, Barbados remains one of the most stable Caribbean islands, with one of the highest standards of living in the region. Since Tom Adams's death in 1985, the political parties have alternated in office and, while the politicians are regarded with increasing scepticism – as everywhere – there is little doubt that prosperity is increasing across the board as the country heads into the new millennium.

Cricket

If you're in Barbados for any length of time, you'll find it almost impossible to avoid the subject of **cricket**; more, perhaps, than anywhere else on earth, the game is *the* national passion. Alongside Jamaica and Trinidad, the island is one of the Big Three Caribbean cricketing nations but, while success in football and athletics has diverted attention from the game in the other two countries, Bajans remain solidly focused on cricket. A measure of the importance of the game was shown in the nation's challenge to a Rest of the World team, played at Bridgetown Oval in March 1967, featuring as one of the key celebrations of the island's newly won independence.

Cricket was first brought to the island by the British military in the second half of the nineteenth century. In 1877, the **Wanderers** became the first cricket club and, for the next few decades, this and the other main clubs reflected the island's racial structure – strictly whites-only and often little more than extended social clubs for the planters and merchants. But despite the snobbery of the top clubs, the

The rules of cricket

The laws of cricket are so complex that the official rule book runs to some twenty pages. The basics, however, are by no means as Byzantine as the game's detractors make out.

There are two teams of eleven players. A team wins by scoring more runs than the other team and dismissing all the opposition – in other words, a team could score many runs more than the opposition, but still not win if the last enemy batsman doggedly stays "in" (hence ensuring a draw). The match is divided into innings, when one team bats and the other fields. The number of innings varies depending on the type of competition: one-day matches have one per team, Test matches have two.

The aim of the fielding side is to limit the runs scored and get the batsmen "out". Two players from the batting side are on the pitch at any one time. The bowling side has a bowler, a wicketkeeper and nine fielders. Two umpires, one standing behind the stumps at the bowler's end and one square onto the play, are responsible for adjudicating if a batsman is out. Each innings is divided into overs, consisting of six deliveries, after which the wicketkeeper changes ends, the bowler is changed and the fielders move positions.

The batsmen score runs either by running up and down from wicket to wicket (one length = one run), or by hitting the ball over the boundary rope, scoring four runs if it crosses the boundary having touched the ground, and six runs if it flies over. The main ways a batsman can be dismissed are: by being "clean bowled", where the bowler dislodges the bails of the wicket (the horizontal pieces of wood resting on top of the stumps); by being "run out", which is when one of the fielding side dislodges the bails with the ball while the batsman is running between the wickets; by being caught, which is when any of the fielding side catches the ball after the batsman has hit it and before it touches the ground; or "lbw" (leg before wicket), where the batsman blocks with his leg a delivery that would otherwise have hit his stumps.

These are the bare rudiments of a game whose beauty lies in the subtlety of its skills and tactics. The captain, for example, chooses which bowler to play and where to position his fielders to counter the strengths of the batsman, the condition of the pitch and a dozen other variables. Cricket also has a beauty in its esoteric language, used to describe such things as fielding positions ("silly mid-off", "cover point", etc) and the various types of bowling delivery ("googly", "yorker", etc).

game had also begun to catch on in the sugar estates, where the workers drew up their own pitches and organized their own matches. In the 1930s the **Barbados Cricket League** was formed to arrange competitions between these mostly rural clubs, helping to spread enthusiasm for the game all over the island and pushing it to new heights.

By the 1950s players from Barbados dominated the West Indies team, whose batting was led by the formidable Bajan 3Ws: **Sir Clyde Walcott**, **Sir Frank Worrell** and **Everton Weekes**. In 1960, Worrell became the side's first ever non-white captain. For several decades the island continued to hold sway over West Indian cricket, with brilliant cricketers like **Sir Gary Sobers**, **Gordon Greenidge** and **Wes Hall** leading the way. And, although the 1980s saw greater success and international representation for smaller islands like Antigua, Barbados remains one of the leading sides in the region and an enduring nursery for world-class players.

Books

Hilary Beckles, *A History of Barbados* (Cambridge University Press). Beckles is the country's leading historian and has produced an excellent and very readable history of the island from the Amerindians to independence.

Edward Braithwaite, *Mother Poem* and *Sun Poem* (Oxford University Press). Highly influential poet, who writes vividly and with passion on a range of themes, from growing up in remote parts of Barbados to the social costs of modern development and his pride in the heritage that the island shares with Africa.

Timothy Callender, *It So Happen* (Heinemann). Humorous and pointed collection of short stories by one of the island's leading writers, featuring the various characters and eccentrics to be found in the archetypal Bajan village.

W.P. Drury, *A Regency Rascal* (o/p). Biography of the dashing but reputedly deceitful Sam Lord, whose "castle" on the southeast coast is one of the island's architectural highlights.

Henry Fraser, *Treasures of Barbados* (Macmillan). Lovingly written and lavishly illustrated history of Bajan architecture, from slave hut and chattel house to the Bridgetown Garrison and the great plantation houses.

Henry Fraser (and others), *A-Z of Barbadian Heritage* (Heinemann Caribbean). A dictionary of everything Bajan, and an essential reference book for anyone with a passion for the island.

F.A. Hoyos, *Tom Adams* (Macmillan). Solid biography of Adams, prime minister from 1976 to 1985, and the best place to look for an overview of political and social change in postwar Barbados.

Eugene Kaplan, *Field Guide to the Coral Reefs of the Caribbean* (Peterson's). Useful introduction to everything you'll find in the sea around Barbados.

George Lamming, *In the Castle of my Skin* (Longman). The outstanding Bajan novel, evoking a nostalgic and beautifully described picture of the island that belonged to former generations.

Patrick Leigh Fermor, *The Traveller's Tree* (Penguin). The classic Caribbean travelogue describing the author's visit in the 1940s, before tourism had really started in the region, though only one of the chapters covers his time on Barbados.

G.W. Lennox & S.A. Seddon, *Flowers of the Caribbean* and *Trees of the Caribbean* (both Macmillan). Handy pocket-sized books, with glossy, sharp, colour pictures, and a good general introduction to the region's flora.

Michael Manley, *A History of West Indies Cricket* (Deutsch). A superb history of the Caribbean contribution to the world's greatest game, engagingly written by the late prime minister of Jamaica.

David Weeks, *Walking Barbados* (Barbados National Trust). 34 island walks, complete with maps, anecdotes and the occasional photo.

Rachel Wilder (ed), *Barbados: the Insight Guide* (APA). Glossy guide, short on practical information but long on colour photographs and features, making it a decent souvenir book.

INDEX

Stay in touch with us!

ROUGHNEWS is Rough Guides' free
newsletter.
In three issues a year we give you
news, travel issues, music reviews,
readers' letters and the latest
dispatches from authors on the road.

I would like to receive ROUGH*NEWS*: please put me on your free mailing list.

NAME . . . .

ADDRESS . . . .

Please clip or photocopy and send to: Rough Guides, 1 Mercer Street, London
WC2H 9QJ, England

or Rough Guides, 375 Hudson Street, New York, NY 10014, USA.

Backpacking through **Europe**?

Cruising across the **US** of **A**?

Clubbing in **London**?

Trekking through **Costa Rica**?

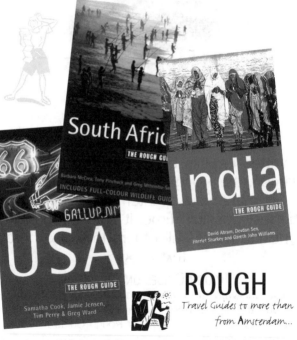

South Afric
THE ROUGH GU
Barbara McCrea, Tony Pinchuck and Greg Mthembu-Sa
INCLUDES FULL-COLOUR WILDLIFE GUIDE

India
THE ROUGH GUIDE
*David Abram, Devdan Sen,
Harriet Sharkey and Gareth John Williams*

USA
THE ROUGH GUIDE
*Samatha Cook, Jamie Jensen,
Tim Perry & Greg Ward*

ROUGH
Travel Guides to more than
from Amsterdam...

NOTES

MAP LIST

MAP SYMBOLS

═══════	Major road	🏛	Stately home
···········	Minor road	♦	Museum
─────	Waterway	⚑	Golf course
─ · · ─	Parish boundary	◠	Cave
▬▬	Church (town maps)	▲	Peak
✝	Church (regional maps)	✈	Airport
✡	Synagogue	■	Places to eat and drink

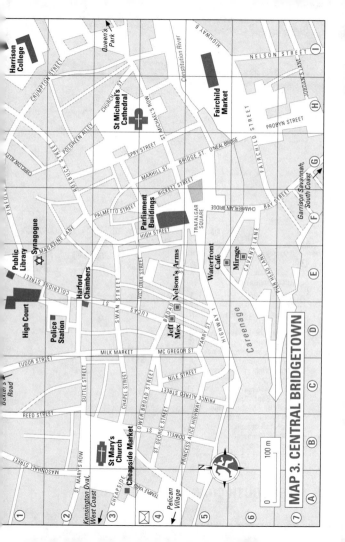

MAP 3. CENTRAL BRIDGETOWN

0 100 m

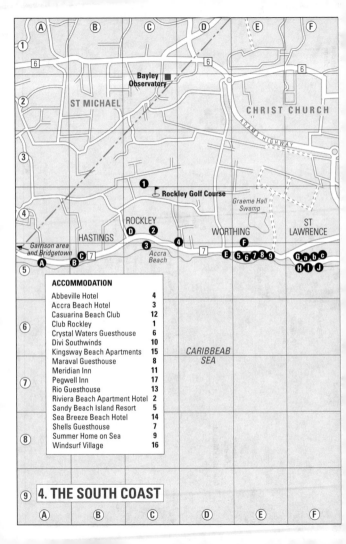

ACCOMMODATION

Abbeville Hotel	4
Accra Beach Hotel	3
Casuarina Beach Club	12
Club Rockley	1
Crystal Waters Guesthouse	6
Divi Southwinds	10
Kingsway Beach Apartments	15
Maraval Guesthouse	8
Meridian Inn	11
Pegwell Inn	17
Rio Guesthouse	13
Riviera Beach Apartment Hotel	2
Sandy Beach Island Resort	5
Sea Breeze Beach Hotel	14
Shells Guesthouse	7
Summer Home on Sea	9
Windsurf Village	16

4. THE SOUTH COAST

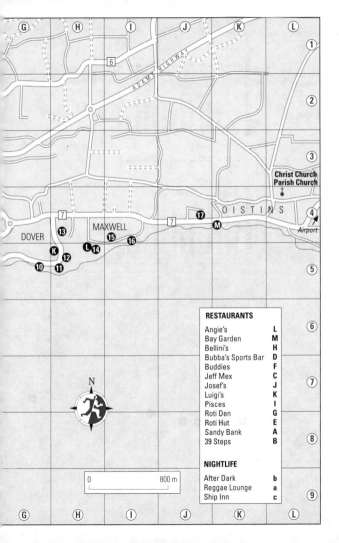

RESTAURANTS

Angie's	**L**
Bay Garden	**M**
Bellini's	**H**
Bubba's Sports Bar	**D**
Buddies	**F**
Jeff Mex	**C**
Josef's	**J**
Luigi's	**K**
Pisces	**I**
Roti Den	**G**
Roti Hut	**E**
Sandy Bank	**A**
39 Steps	**B**

NIGHTLIFE

After Dark	**b**
Reggae Lounge	**a**
Ship Inn	**c**

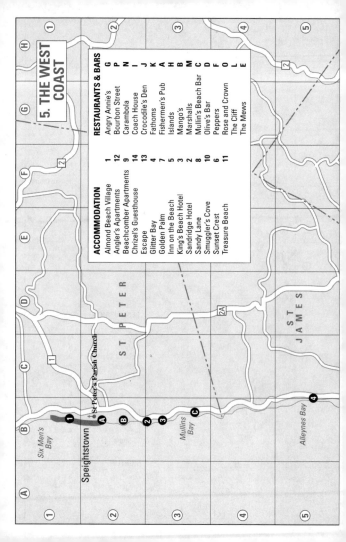

5. THE WEST COAST

ACCOMMODATION

Almond Beach Village	1
Angler's Apartments	12
Beachcomber Apartments	9
Chrizel's Guesthouse	14
Escape	13
Glitter Bay	4
Golden Palm	7
Inn on the Beach	5
King's Beach Hotel	3
Sandridge Hotel	2
Sandy Lane	8
Smuggler's Cove	10
Sunset Crest	6
Treasure Beach	11

RESTAURANTS & BARS

Angry Annie's	G
Bourbon Street	P
Carambola	N
Coach House	I
Crocodile's Den	J
Fathoms	K
Fishermen's Pub	A
Islands	H
Mango's	B
Marshalls	M
Mullin's Beach Bar	C
Olive's Bar	D
Peppers	F
Rose and Crown	O
The Cliff	L
The Mews	E

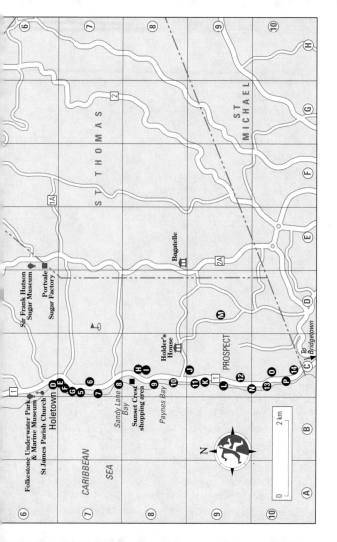